GREAT WAR
LITERATURE

A-LEVEL STUDY GUIDE

Written by W Lawrance

on

STRANGE MEETING

A NOVEL BY SUSAN HILL

Great War Literature A-Level Study Guide on Strange Meeting, a novel by Susan Hill.
Written by W Lawrance

Published by:
Great War Literature Publishing LLP
Darrington Lodge, Springfield Road, Camberley, Surrey GU15 1AB Great Britain
Web site: *www.greatwarliterature.co.uk*
E-Mail: *editor@greatwarliterature.co.uk*

Produced in Great Britain

ISBN 978-1905378456 (1905378459) Revised Edition in Paperback - September 2008
Replaces version published in Paperback 2005 (ISBN: 1905378210)

10 9 8 7 6 5 4 3 2 1

Design and production by Great War Literature Publishing LLP
Typeset in Neue Helvetica, ITC Berkeley Old Style and Trajan Pro

Great War Literature A-Level Study Guide on

Strange Meeting

CONTENTS

Preface	5
Introduction	7
Synopsis	9
1. Part One	9
2. Part Two	16
3. Part Three	22
Character Analysis	27
1. John Hilliard	27
2. David Barton	34
3. Colonel Garrett	39
4. Captain Franklin	42
5. Constance Hilliard	44
6. Beth Hilliard	46
Themes and Comparisons	49
1. Portrayal of Love	49
2. The Effects of War on the Individual	55
3. The Home Front	61
4. Hope	66
Critical Analysis	71
1. Inconsistencies	71
2. Narrative Style	74
Coursework Assistance	79
1. Essay Suggestions	79
2. Comparative Work	90
Further Reading Recommendations	97
Bibliography	105
Other Titles	107

Preface

The primary purpose of Great War Literature Study Guides is to provide in-depth analysis of First World War literature for GCSE and A-Level students.

Great War Literature Publishing have taken the positive decision to produce a uniquely detailed and in-depth interpretation of selected works for students. We also actively promote the publication of our works in an electronic format via the Internet to give the broadest possible access.

Our publications can be used in isolation or in collaboration with other study guides. It is our aim to provide assistance with your understanding of First World War literature, not to provide the answers to specific questions. This approach provides the resources that allow the student the freedom to reach their own conclusions and express an independent viewpoint.

The structure of Great War Literature Study Guides allows the reader to delve into a required section easily without the need to read from beginning to end.

The Great War Literature Study Guides have been thoroughly researched and are the result of over 25 years of experience of studying this particular genre.

Studying literature is not about being right or wrong, it is entirely a matter of opinion. The secret to success is developing the ability to form these opinions and to deliver them succinctly and reinforce them with quotes and clear references from the text.

Great War Literature Study Guides help to extend your knowledge of First World War literature and offer clear definitions and guidance to enhance your studying. Our clear and simple layouts make the guides easy to access and understand.

The Great War Literature A-Level Study Guide on *Strange Meeting*, provides a critical assessment of many aspects of this novel and is based entirely on the opinion of the author of this guide.

INTRODUCTION

Strange Meeting is a remarkable, beautiful and moving book. It tells the story of two young men, from very different backgrounds, who, on the surface, have little in common. They meet in the most difficult circumstances, on the Western Front in the late summer of 1916, yet they manage to rise above their surroundings by forming a deep and lasting friendship. It is not so much the war, as the development of their relationship, which forms the basis for this novel.

Upon reading this text, the reader easily becomes absorbed into the lives of these two men and their comrades. One shares their feelings and fears, their desperation to survive and enjoy the remainder of their lives, their everyday discomforts and amusements. The sights, sounds and even smells which they witness, are evocatively and descriptively brought to life throughout the pages of this novel.

This is still, however, a story of a war and its effects - physical, emotional and psychological. While there are no graphic descriptions of battles, wounds and death, the conflict is omnipresent. It is also, and perhaps more importantly, a story of love, both conventional and 'forbidden'; of human relationships of every variety. This novel shows how, despite the most hideous losses, it is always possible to become a better, more fulfilled person, and above all, to have hope for the future.

Susan Hill has said in her 'Afterword' that she felt that, while writing the novel, Hilliard and Barton had come to represent the many thousands of young men who gave their lives in this devastating conflict and that she had written the novel in honour of men such as these. This novel represents a fitting and true memorial to them.

I have absolutely no hesitation in stating that, in my opinion and considerable experience, *Strange Meeting* is probably the finest First World War novel which has been written to date. Susan Hill's treatment of her subject and characters is sympathetic and realistic without being overly sentimental. In *Strange Meeting* she demonstrates man's astounding capacity for love, tolerance and compassion, despite, or sometimes because of, his surroundings. This, quite simply, is a story told during the worst of times, about the very best of men.

W Lawrance
September 2008

STRANGE MEETING

BY SUSAN HILL

SYNOPSIS

PART ONE

It is the summer of 1916. John Hilliard is on convalescent leave, having been
wounded in the leg at the beginning of the Battle of the Somme. He is staying
at his parents' house on the coast, recovering from his injury. He is unable to
sleep properly and, on the night before he is due to return to France, he lies
awake remembering his time in hospital when he was first injured. The
memories of the sights and sounds of the men around him all come flooding
back, together with his meeting with a childhood acquaintance, named
Crawford, who is serving in France in a hospital behind the lines. Hilliard
feels resentment towards Crawford because of his non-combatant status, even
though he knows this is unreasonable - after all, someone must tend to the
wounded and dying.

In the hospital, Hilliard had been unable to sleep because of all the noises of
men suffering and the general disturbances in the ward. Now he is at home,
he has no desire to sleep. He tries to force himself to stay awake and thinks
about his homecoming. He feels he does not belong with his family any
more. He knows that he has changed while everything in England has
remained the same. Eventually, however, exhaustion overwhelms him and he
sleeps. Then the dreams begin. At first they are relatively happy as he dreams
of his sister Beth and the relationship which they used to share. Then there
are the nightmares in which he has visions of piles of corpses. He wakes
suddenly, feeling sick and remembering that the following day he will return
to France. This thought leaves him feeling contented - he wants to go back.

Although it is still the early hours of the morning, he rises and goes for a walk on the beach. He thinks about how out of touch the people at home are with the reality of the war. His parents, sister and even the Major (a family friend) are full of complacency and sometimes arrogance about the conflict. They have all formed their own opinions, based on newspaper reports and hearsay, but have no idea and little interest in what is really happening in France. He thinks he can hear the thudding of the guns in the distance, but wonders whether this is just his imagination playing tricks. Then, he recalls childhood events with Beth - memories of calmer and happier days, when she had protected and helped him.

He returns to the house and wakes his sister, believing that he wants to explain his feelings to her - to unburden himself and tell her what the war is *really* like. Unsure of how to begin, he hesitates and Beth takes this opportunity to tell him that she is going to marry a lawyer named Henry Partington - a man twice her age, widowed, with one son. John's moment is lost, as he realises that Beth has also changed and that he can no longer confide in her. Although he is initially confused by her choice of husband, John soon comes to understand that Beth is taking the only option available to her if she wants to marry and leave home.

Having prepared to leave for his return journey to France, John reluctantly agrees to allow his mother to accompany him to the railway station. As they await the train, Constance Hilliard comments on the poor condition of the platform, stating that Kemble, the stationmaster, has allowed standards to deteriorate. She slips into the conversation, almost as an afterthought, that Kemble's son has been killed at Mons. John cannot understand her misplaced priorities and this reinforces his belief that he no longer belongs at home. Constance tells John that his departure reminds her of when he used to leave for boarding school as a child, and that she copes with his absence by not allowing herself to worry. The train departs and John is finally able to relax a little.

In London, he does some shopping; he has promised to take various items back to France for some of the other men. He buys himself a new cane which makes him feel conspicuously like an inexperienced soldier and he wants to tell people that he is *not* a new recruit - he has been to France and seen the realities of war. He goes to Victoria Station three hours early, still feeling remote and cut-off from everything around him. Gradually, however, he begins to feel much more relaxed and at peace - he looks forward to being able to stop worrying and return to the simplicity of life in the trenches: following and giving orders; making decisions, with nobody questioning his every move. He is happy - he feels that he is going "home".

On the boat, he sleeps - and, for once, he does not dream. When he alights from the train in France, he is met, not by his batman Bates, whom he had been expecting, but by a man named Coulter. Bates, it would seem, has been killed. Coulter gathers together the reinforcements who have also arrived on the train and they begin the walk to the rest camp where Hilliard's battalion are billeted. Coulter tells Hilliard that, during his absence, they have suffered high casualties and that he will struggle to find a familiar face amongst the officers and men.

Upon reaching his billet, Hilliard is angry to discover that he must share both Coulter and his accommodation with another subaltern - Second Lieutenant David Barton. He had been looking forward to being alone again and resents this intrusion into his privacy.

He does not get to meet Barton immediately, as he must report to the Commanding Officer, Colonel Garrett. Hilliard finds that Garrett has changed - he is now complaining, fidgety and agitated. Gone is the calm and unflustered man that Hilliard remembers. Garrett tells Hilliard of the horrors he has missed, painting a picture of confusion; a battle gone horribly wrong; delayed orders; faulty equipment; men being shot and blown up; men being mown down by their own guns; no relief. He also tells the story of a man named Clifford, who went mad and shot himself. Hilliard is worried now: can Garrett be relied upon? He seems to have lost his nerve and Hilliard notices that he is drinking heavily.

When he returns to his billet, Hilliard finds David Barton waiting for him. Barton seems a likeable man, but Hilliard immediately feels ill-at-ease, particularly about David's ability to speak so openly. Later, Barton amuses the officers over dinner, with tales of family and home. Gradually, Hilliard begins to warm to him and realises that Barton has qualities which the other men lack. He is unsure whether it is Barton's innocence, or his youth, or another quality altogether, but whatever it is, he knows - quite suddenly - that they all need this young man to remain exactly as he is, to not lose any of these qualities.

After dinner, the two officers go for a walk. Barton talks openly about himself and all his family. This is something which Hilliard has always considered impossible as it would mean revealing too much of himself. But, in Barton's company and, with his gentle encouragement, he realises that he can talk; in fact he discovers that he has been waiting for someone with whom to share his thoughts. His anxiety fades and he feels a strange sense of peace and contentment.

When they return to their billet, Barton asks Hilliard how he came to be injured. Hilliard explains to Barton what happened, then retires to bed. Memories of the hospital come flashing back to him. He remembers the man in the next bed and how he had been unable to offer any help, even though all this man had wanted was to talk to someone. This remembrance heightens Hilliard's sense of emotional inadequacy. Barton immediately senses that something is wrong, but does not force the issue, offering Hilliard some brandy to calm his nerves. Hilliard desperately wants to explain to Barton, to tell him what has happened and release the tension in his own mind. However, he is overcome by tiredness. Just before he goes to sleep he also realises that he wants to protect Barton and keep him safe from the war, partly because he knows that the young subaltern has so much to offer to the men, but also because *he* needs Barton.

One evening, the two men go into the nearest town, where life seems to be carrying on as though there is no war - except that there are no young men to be seen, other than the soldiers. They listen to music and enjoy themselves, inviting Captain Franklin to join them. The Captain refuses this offer, which makes Hilliard angry, but Barton remains contented - as always. He also writes very long, detailed letters to his family, full of jokes and fond remembrances. Hilliards' letters home are a complete contrast - being short, reserved and polite. Gradually, Barton's relations start sending messages to Hilliard in their letters and he is slowly introduced to a close and loving family for the first time.

Captain Franklin suggests that Barton should be sent on a gas course. Garrett asks Hilliard's opinion and despite the fact that it would mean a week of safety for Barton behind the lines, Hilliard says that he thinks that Barton should remain with the Company, because they 'need him'. Garrett is forced to agree and Barton stays. Hilliard later realises that, as much as he wants Barton to be safe, the idea of being separated from his new friend is too much for him to contemplate. He also begins to understand that Franklin dislikes both himself and Barton, although his reasons are unclear. Back with Barton, Hilliard voices his concerns about Franklin's attitude, but Barton remains easy-going, despite Hilliard's warnings that Franklin could, if he chose, make things difficult for them when they get back into the trenches.

Orders come for the battalion to move up to the front lines. Their work and packing done Hilliard and Barton decide to walk down to the nearby orchard. Just as they are about to leave, Franklin calls them back and tells them that Barton will have to walk on the following day's march, as there are not enough horses for all the officers. Hilliard is angry again, believing that Franklin is purposely trying to keep them apart. As they walk to the orchard, Barton smells burning and runs towards its source: the wreckage of a German aeroplane. Upon closer inspection, they discover the charred remains of the pilot. Hilliard feels saddened that the war and its horrors have returned so soon. Then he sees Barton's face and realises that, having witnessed this scene, his young friend will never be quite the same again. This is Barton's first experience of death in the war and Hilliard has an overwhelming sense of pity mingled with a continued desire to protect him. Barton, however, is more realistic. He knows that for him, as for everyone, the peace could not last forever and that the awfulness of the war had to start eventually.

Main Points of Interest in Part One

HILLIARD AT HOME

- A valuable insight into John Hilliard's character as well as the home front.

- Susan Hill creates an atmosphere of heat and brooding tension, even though John is far away from danger.

- Hilliard is unhappy at home and desperate to return to the front - which he now considers to be his 'home'.

- Beth and Constance Hilliard are the only female characters we actually meet in the novel.

BARTON IS INTRODUCED

- Although Hilliard is initially angry about having to share his accommodation with another man, this soon passes, as Barton's easy-going personality captivates him.

- It is not just Hilliard who is affected by the presence of David Barton. Everyone, except Captain Franklin, seems to benefit from knowing him and he brings a sense of relief to the assembled Company.

- Barton's family are also introduced in his letters and, almost immediately, Hilliard becomes involved in their correspondence. Their attitude is a contrast with his own family's detachment.

- Hilliard's attachment to Barton grows throughout this first part, from initial distrust, to a deep desire never to be parted from his new friend.

OTHER CHARACTERS

- Colonel Garrett is shown to be war-weary and deeply troubled, depending on alcohol to control his nerves.
- Captain Franklin is efficient, but cold. He seems to have a deep distrust of Barton and Hilliard, although the reasons behind this are not made clear.
- Coulter is portrayed as showing full-hearted support for the war, but with a lively sense of fun.

RETURN TO WAR

- The war plays a very small part in this section of the novel, which has more to do with creating atmosphere and building characters, but at the end, the men receive orders to march back towards the front.
- This will be Barton's first experience of war and Hilliard realises that he desperately wants to protect his new friend from the truths which await him.

PART TWO

During the march to the front, Barton and Hilliard are separated - Hilliard must ride, while Barton walks. Barton thinks of Hilliard's detached family, comparing them with his own; and also of their first meeting when he had instinctively known that he and Hilliard would be friends. As they enter their destination town of Feuvry, Hilliard rides by and sees Barton's face. He witnesses a look of shock on the face of his new friend, such as he had not seen when Barton had looked upon the body of the dead German pilot. Hilliard realises that, just like the demolished town before them, Barton's innocence is being destroyed.

Barton writes letters home but the tone has changed from contained excitement to shock, as he describes the ruined town of Feuvry to his family. He seems aware and slightly resentful of the fact that Hilliard is trying to protect him from the realities of war and points out that he is already bothered by the noise of the guns, although they are still some distance away.

That night, in their billet, a sergeant comes and asks if the two lieutenants can help him with a man called Harris who has shut himself in a cellar and is refusing to come out. Initially, as the more experienced officer, Hilliard takes control, although Barton feels aggrieved that he is denied the opportunity of proving himself. After a while, however, Hillard reappears. He needs Barton's assistance. He knows that Barton is better suited to this task, in that he will be able to talk to Harris and communicate better than Hilliard could. Harris, a young inexperienced soldier is terrified and his fear begins to make Barton feel more afraid about going up to the front. Eventually, however, Barton persuades Harris to come out of the cellar and takes him back upstairs. He tells Harris to wait on a landing, while he goes to fetch some alcohol to sooth the young soldier's nerves. Just before he reaches his room, a shell hits the building and Harris is killed. In total, nine men are killed in the blast.

Barton is wracked with guilt and Hilliard, grateful that Barton himself survived the shelling, tells him that this is what the war is like. He suggests that Barton should undertake to write to Harris's family, believing that this may help him to come to terms with what has happened. Hilliard notices that Barton has changed: he looks shocked, miserable and exhausted. He tells

Barton how afraid he had been that Barton himself had been killed in the blast, how much he has come to depend on the younger man for support and how much he needs him.

Barton writes a long letter to his family, which starts off in a depressed tone of tiredness and indifference. Gradually, as he writes, he becomes more cheerful. Two weeks are spent in the support trenches and Barton, in common with many of the men, becomes fidgety. He is beginning to yearn for excitement. Hilliard merely feels settled and contented, relaxed in the knowledge that he and Barton have become so comfortable in each other's company. Encouraged by their son, the Barton family send letters directly to Hilliard, who is touched by their kindness. Slowly, Hilliard's feelings for his friend become even deeper and his need for Barton to survive is now almost overwhelming.

Barton is ordered up to the front line to make a map and bring back information. He is pleased and proud to be given this assignment but Hilliard, on the other hand, is desperately worried, once again, that Barton may not survive. He feels confused about his feelings towards Barton as these emotions are strange to him. Just before Barton leaves, he realises that the feeling he is experiencing is love. Despite the serious implications of this thought, the admission of his feelings, even if only to himself, makes him feel more calm. But then, panic sets in again - what will he do if Barton is killed?

Barton is collected from the dugout by a man named Grosse, who will guide him through the communication trenches into the front line. Garrett sends for Hilliard, who is grateful to be away from the dugout, rather than having to sit there and wait anxiously for Barton's return. Garrett tells Hilliard, unofficially, that they are about to move into the front line trenches. Both men understand that this will mean hard work for the men and, worst of all, reconnaissance raids, which they know will prove to be a waste of lives. After a while, Garrett remarks that Barton should, by now, have reached the front line, reminding Hilliard of his fears. At the same time, however, Hilliard realises that Garrett has asked him to Headquarters so that he will not have to sit alone in the dugout, worrying about Barton. They discuss Barton briefly and Garrett shows his perception when he points out that this new officer has qualities which the rest of them lack and that they *all* need him. Hilliard experiences a sense of pride that their Commanding Officer appreciates and values Barton's qualities.

Meanwhile, Barton is making his way through the trenches to the observation post with Grosse, when a shell lands just ahead of him. He rounds a corner to find a terrifying scene of mutilation. Stretcher bearers arrive and before long Barton and Gross are able to continue on their way. A little further on, a private is shot by a sniper and dies right in front of Barton. Suddenly he is overwhelmed by the pointlessness and futility of the war: he has been sent out to the front line to draw a map, while all around him young men are dying and his map won't help them or anyone else. In a moment of calm, detached insanity, Barton stands up, with his head above the parapet until Grosse angrily drags him back down to safety again. They carry on with their mission, but Barton knows that, for him, everything will be different from now on.

Hilliard notices that Barton has altered as soon as he returns. Their orders have been changed and they are now housed in tents further back, behind the lines. Barton's personality is now completely different: gone are his openness and warmth and in their place are apathy and silence. Over a week after his expedition into the front line, he still refuses to discuss his assignment - in fact he barely talks at all and Hilliard feels isolated and helpless. He suggests that Barton might prefer to billet with another of the officers and Barton's response is apathetic - he does not seem to care where he sleeps. He just sits quietly and writes. This time, however, he is not writing a letter. Later, Hilliard reads what Barton has been writing - extracts from a book which seem to question whether it would be easier to die or to carry on living, and does that decision depend on the quality of the life you are left with? Despite reading Barton's notes, Hilliard still cannot understand what his friend is thinking. Barton seems to neither know nor care what he is doing and Hilliard feels, once again, that he has failed the younger man. They go to Battalion Headquarters to receive their orders and Hilliard feels intensely jealous of the fact the Barton can still talk and laugh with the other officers and yet remains aloof with him. They discover they are to go back to the front the next day.

That night, Hilliard wakes to hear a tearing sound. Barton has ripped his book and his notes to shreds. He explains that he had been trying to make sense of everything around him but has decided that this is impossible, because nothing makes sense. Hilliard is relieved - at least Barton is talking to him again. Barton pours out his feelings: his anger about the deaths he has witnessed and the futility of the war. He also speaks about his feeling of numbness and reveals that he is worried that he has stopped being able to feel or care about anything. Hilliard reassures him: the fact that he is able to talk about it means he *does* care - he must, otherwise, he would not bother to mention it, or to get so upset; he should not be surprised or ashamed at the feelings he is now experiencing. It takes some considerable time, but the two men are eventually able to relax with each other again. Barton then takes the enormous step of telling Hilliard that he loves him.

Main Points of Interest in Part Two

DEATH OF HARRIS

- Harris is not a character to whom we have been introduced, but his death becomes Barton's first real experience of war.

- The pointlessness of Harris's death frightens Barton and Hilliard wants to help him to understand that there is no point in trying to make sense of the war.

- This episode marks the first time during which Hilliard has really had to contemplate losing Barton.

BUILDING THE RELATIONSHIP

- The relationship between Barton and Hilliard is developed, especially following Harris's death.

- The characters are evolved: Barton's long letter home reveals how the episode at Feuvry has affected him. The conversations between the two men demonstrate their growing mutual dependence and affection.

HILLIARD FACES HIS OWN FEELINGS

- The news that Barton will have to go into the front line forces Hilliard to face up to how much Barton really means to him.

- In accepting that, without Barton he would be lost, Hilliard also realises that, probably for the first time in his life, he is in love.

BARTON'S EXPERIENCE IN THE FRONT LINE

- Witnessing death at such close quarters forces Barton to question his own outlook on the war.

- When he returns, he cannot face Hilliard and refuses to communicate any more than is strictly necessary, although he continues to speak freely to other officers.

- A wall of silence builds up between the two men and Hilliard lacks the ability to break it down.

REBUILDING THE RELATIONSHIP

- Having reached the point of despair, Hilliard finally manages to pierce the silence between the two men.
- He allows Barton to understand that it is perfectly normal to have a bad reaction to witnessing death and, that to do so proves that he is not callous or inhuman, but exactly the opposite.
- Their affection restored, Barton solemnly declares his love for Hilliard - which is clearly and gladly reciprocated.

PART THREE

This opens with a long letter from Barton to his family. He gives them a great deal of detail about the day-to-day horrors of trench life: rats, lice, rain, death and also of the changes the war has made to him personally, although he glosses over his recent feelings regarding the war, telling them that such thoughts are in the past. He acknowledges how much he misses home and how important Hilliard has become to him. From this letter, we also learn that the Battalion has moved to different location, that they have been experiencing very bad weather and have come under heavy bombardments.

Hilliard receives a very formal letter from Beth telling him that she is shortly to marry Henry Partington. Barton is stunned by the abrupt tone of Beth's letter. That night, Hilliard and Barton are ordered to gather together a party of men and carry out a reconnaissance of the enemy trenches. They come under heavy fire and are forced back to their own trench. Three men are dead, including Coulter, whom they have been forced to abandon in No Man's Land due to his appalling injuries. When they get back to their own trench, Hilliard is initially angry with Barton because he (Barton) went too close to the enemy lines and gave away their position. However, when Captain Franklin questions Hilliard about the the raid, Hilliard plays down the incident and does not mention Barton's error. Later, he tries to reassure Barton that, even if it was his fault, it was an easy mistake to make being as it was his first time in No Man's Land, and that he should not blame himself.

Barton writes home that he is haunted by what has happened - particularly leaving Coulter in No Man's Land: he is worried that Coulter isn't really dead and believes that there is a possibility that he wasn't that badly wounded after all. Again, however, he is convinced that Hilliard is trying to protect him from the reality of what happened to their batman. He is also shocked by some of his own behaviour: he remembers that he risked his life to save a hedgehog from No Man's Land and contrasts this with the fact that he had not even attempted to save Coulter.

Hilliard and Barton are ordered, along with the other officers, to attend a meeting with Garrett who tells them that he has refused to order any further reconnaissance raids, which he deems unnecessary and pointless. As a result of taking this stance, he has been relieved of his command and ordered back to England. By now it is the end of November 1916. Garrett is replaced by Colonel Keene who is soft-spoken and apparently hesitant, but has a reputation for thoroughness.

The men receive orders to go into battle and, the night before the attack, Barton reveals how frightened he is. Hilliard reassures him that this is perfectly normal, before Barton goes out into the trenches to get some fresh air. In the trench he meets, and briefly talks with a man named Parkin. A year younger than Barton, Parkin is equally inexperienced and nervous about the forthcoming battle. Back in the dugout, Barton is still afraid, so he and Hilliard discuss the future; they plan to spend Christmas together, if possible, with Barton's family. They talk about what lies ahead for them. Just before they sleep, they speak about their unique love for one another.

Next morning, Barton's fears of the previous night have dissipated, but Hilliard feels a strong sense of foreboding about his friend. The barrage begins at eight o'clock. Eventually they go over the top but Barton and Hilliard are quickly separated. They come under heavy enemy fire and Hilliard soon realises that the attack is hopeless and that the men are being mown down by gunfire. The battlefield is in chaos. Hilliard meets Parkin and they seek shelter in a shell-hole. Hilliard notices that his leg is injured and Parkin offers to go for help. Alone in the shell-hole, Hilliard drifts in and out of consciousness. He dreams disjointedly of Barton and Beth. In his more lucid moments, he hears the cries of other wounded men, but no-one comes to help him. He decides that he must get back to the trench, because he needs to know what has happened to Barton. He drags himself out of the shell-hole, picking his way between the dead bodies, one of which is Parkin, who had gone barely a few yards out of the shell-hole before being killed.

It takes him until the middle of the next morning to get back to his own lines, but he's at the wrong end of the trench and the men here are strangers to him. They send for stretcher-bearers and he is taken away, despite his desperate, but unsuccessful, attempts to get news of Barton.

When Hilliard next wakes, he is in hospital, and Captain Franklin is with him. Hilliard is confused: he doesn't understand what has happened, where he has been or where he is. His left leg has been amputated but he is, initially, unaware of this. Parcels and letters arrive from his family - although these retain the usual formality of all their correspondence. He receives a letter from Barton's mother which he is afraid to open, but eventually after ten days, he accepts that he must. It tells him that Barton has been reported as missing, believed killed. Barton's mother begs Hilliard to give her any information he has and writes in loving, warm language of her concern for him. A second letter from her reveals that Barton's belongings have been forwarded to his family and that they have received a sympathetic letter from Captain Franklin.

Hilliard writes back to Miriam Barton, telling her that David is almost certainly dead. He wants the family to know the truth, because this is what Barton would have wanted. He also promises to visit them when he is well enough. Before long, he returns to England, although he dreads the prospect of facing people and cannot reconcile himself to the fact that Barton is dead.

Initially, he is sent to a convalescent home where he is visited by his mother. He asks her to send him copies of the books which Barton had been reading, although when they arrive, he cannot bring himself to read them. Colonel Garrett visits, but they find little to discuss. Hilliard's only thoughts are of Barton: he feels remote from everything else - even the loss of his own leg. Barton's family write and tell him they are looking forward to his visit and are finalising plans. They are full of concern for his wellbeing.

When Hilliard is sufficiently recovered, he visits Barton's home. Everything is exactly as Barton had described it. So vivid were his descriptions, that Hilliard feels as though he has been here before. Finally, he seems to believe in something and looks ahead to the future.

Main Points of Interest in Part Three

RECONNAISSANCE RAID

- Not only does this raid signify the death of Coulter, it also marks Barton's first experience in No Man's Land.
- Hilliard's anger with Barton shows how shocking the whole experience had been.
- Despite his own misgivings, Hilliard still defends Barton and tries to reassure him after the raid.

COLONEL GARRETT LEAVES

- Following the raid, and having received orders to carry out more, Garrett refuses to obey and is sent home in disgrace.
- Barton and Hilliard view this departure differently.
- The new colonel arrives, but the relationship will not be the same as with Garrett.

THE ATTACK

- During the night before the attack, the conversation between Barton and Hilliard proves how deep their affection has become.
- Hilliard does everything he can to alleviate Barton's fears, which do eventually pass.
- They part in the trench before the raid begins and do not see each other again.

HILLIARD'S INJURY

- Throughout most of his time in No Man's Land, Hilliard's only concern is to get back to his own trenches and find out what has happened to Barton.

- Hilliard's leg is amputated, meaning that his war is over.

- He still has no confirmed news of Barton's fate, although he probably knows that his friend has not survived.

CONTACT WITH BARTON'S FAMILY

- Hilliard's only real news of Barton comes from his own family, which confirms in his own mind that Barton is dead, although no body has been found.

- Barton's family write often and affectionately to Hilliard and invite him to visit as soon as he is well enough.

- When he is sufficiently recovered, Hilliard fulfils his ambition of seeing Barton's home.

CHARACTER ANALYSIS

Strange Meeting is a novel, which despite its setting, is not really about war: it is about the people who fight the war. As such, the creation of the characters is of the greatest importance and is essential to really understanding the story. In her lead characters, Susan Hill has created two of the most effective, sympathetic and, probably, realistic personalities of First World War fiction so I have devoted most of this section to the construction of these particular characters.

1. JOHN HILLIARD

John Hilliard is a Second Lieutenant in his early twenties (we are told in Part One that in April, upon first arriving in France, he was 22 years old), who, at the beginning of the story, is about to return to his battalion after being on sick leave for five weeks. The beginning of the novel is based around the creation of his character, which the reader discovers through his thoughts and memories of both his childhood and war experiences.

As a young child Hilliard had been very insecure and had relied on his older sister Beth, often sleeping under her bed at night and then, as this was forbidden, creeping back to his own room in the early hours of the morning. His memories of Beth at the beginning of the novel revolve around his dependence upon her and their shared bonds of fellowship. He recalls various aspects of their childhood which reflect her strong influence over him and which allow us to contrast this with her behaviour while he is on leave and also with the tone of her letters, which follow later. Thus, we can see and feel his disappointment with regard to her decision to marry Henry

Partington. Hilliard had hoped that during his leave, he and his sister would be able to spend some time together and that he would be able to explain things about the war, to talk to her and try, through her to gain some understanding for himself. However, he discovers that in his absence, she has become more independent of him and has developed a life of her own.

John Hilliard's upbringing had been typically upper-class and Victorian - staid and devoid of outward displays of affection or emotion. As a result of this, he finds it difficult to communicate, especially when it comes to showing how he feels. He is a reserved character and prefers his own company to being amongst crowds of people, as he finds conversation awkward. Hilliard's taciturn nature is clear from the beginning of the novel, as we learn that he has an unprovoked and inexplicable dislike for Crawford. Even he accepts that these feelings are 'pointless', and are based on childish jealousy and irrational dislike, but he also feels incapable of really changing his viewpoint. He appreciates that Crawford's non-combatant status does not mean that he has an easier life than the men serving at the front, but that does not stop him from harbouring an unreasonable resentment.

His relationship with his mother is complex. He thinks highly of her, appreciating her beauty, but her detached attitude seems to cause him some confusion, even though it actually mirrors his own. He is desperate to be alone and to avoid too much contact with his family, especially since, in his eyes, Beth has changed since they last met. So he shuns situations where he will have to explain himself or his actions to his family, but most especially to his mother. There is no affection between Hilliard and his family, although at the beginning of the novel, this does not really seem to affect him, as he only really wants to return to the front, where he knows that he will feel more relaxed. Hilliard's father is barely mentioned, other than the fact that he devotes a disproportionate amount of time to his garden and that Hilliard's mother seems to be trying to turn her son into a replica of him. As such, it could be said that most of Hilliard's childhood has been influenced by women.

As an officer, Hilliard is well thought-of. We learn that Garrett had been known to frequently confide in Hilliard and has been keenly awaiting his return to the Company. Garrett trusts Hilliard enough to be brutally honest with him about his views on the conduct of the war and everyone seems very pleased to see him return as well as being concerned to ensure that he is now fit again.

Meeting with Barton completely transforms Hilliard's personality - and his life. He is initially wary of this new officer, resenting his presence and, especially, the intrusion into his privacy. Despite the fact that he has never met Barton, Hilliard is 'certain' that he will not like him. However, Barton's easy manner soon puts Hilliard at ease, especially when he reveals that he had been fearful of meeting Hilliard. This level of honesty is quite disarming and makes it almost impossible for Hilliard to think badly of Barton, regardless of the fact that he cannot imagine being so open himself. Under Barton's influence, Hilliard finds that he is able to talk about himself and listen more attentively to others, especially Barton. He begins to look at those around him differently, showing a greater degree of tolerance and understanding.

His relationship with Barton soon changes as he rapidly becomes very concerned for his new friend's welfare. He tries his best to shield Barton from the reality of war, worrying that this will affect him, perhaps more deeply than most, and bring unwelcome changes to his personality. The emotional attachment between the two men is also quickly formed, as Hilliard finds himself immediately able to trust Barton. Many of these feelings are new to Hilliard, but he is determined to pursue the matter and understand as much as he can about Barton.

Barton's family are quick to show Hilliard affection too and, initially, he seems unsure as to how to respond to them. His surprise at their easy acceptance of him shows that he has a low opinion of himself, which is slowly being corrected under Barton's influence. Before long, Hilliard has learned to accept the attentions of Barton's family and even begins to reciprocate. Nevertheless, this new-found openness does not extend to his own family: his letters to them remain distant and matter-of-fact.

Harris's death is the first real problem which the two men have to confront together. Barton feels guilty that he 'caused' Harris to die, while Hilliard simply wants to protect Barton and tries to explain this to him. We are told that Hilliard desperately wants to reach out to Barton, to touch him and help him, but that he cannot. A physical approach is not something with which Hilliard is familiar or comfortable and, unfortunately, Barton is too upset himself to really appreciate that Hilliard is doing his best to connect with him in the only way he can, because he is still learning to deal with these new emotions and show affection.

After this episode, the relationship between Barton and Hilliard develops fairly rapidly, although it must be remembered that they live in extremely close proximity and, therefore, once the initial friendship and affection are established, it is easier for them to become more closely attached than people who see each other less frequently. Barton makes a telling observation in one of his letters, when he says that Hilliard 'doesn't seem to be so afraid of himself', showing that Barton has noticed a change in his friend's personality since their first meeting. Hilliard had probably seemed 'afraid' of his own personality, simply because he was unsure how to react to people and how to behave in the company of the other men, giving him an air of diffidence.

When Barton is chosen to go up to the front line to draw a map, Hilliard becomes desperately worried that something will happen to his friend. He would rather go himself and face the dangers involved than confront the thought of living without Barton. He realises, in a moment of 'absolute clarity' that the feelings which he is experiencing are love. Hilliard has never loved anyone in his life, but he realises immediately that from now on, nothing else will really matter in his life - not the consequences of this love, not the war, not family reactions - only Barton.

It is because of this newly-discovered love that Hilliard is so distressed by Barton's adverse reaction to his experiences in the front-line trench. The rift which is formed between them frustrates Hilliard as he does not really understand how to deal with the situation, resulting in a feeling of extreme helplessness. He even goes so far as to suggest that they should take a 'break' from each other and Barton's slightly apathetic response to this does not help matters. This situation confirms all of Hilliard's worst fears: Barton will lose his innocence and be affected by the war, to such an extent that Hilliard will not be able to help and then they will grow apart. Hilliard, feeling alone and desolate, becomes jealous of the fact that Barton is still capable of talking and laughing with other officers, but seems unable to communicate with Hilliard at all. He wants to keep Barton all to himself and guards against the perceived interference of others, but at the same time, is desperately unhappy himself.

Eventually, Hilliard manages to drag the story out of Barton and make him talk about his experience, partly because his understanding of war has taught him that talking is the best way to recover from shock, but also because this had been Barton's own method to force Hilliard to communicate when they first met. At this point, Hilliard begins to wonder whether there is 'anything that he had not learned from David.' By communicating, they are able to break down the temporary barrier which has arisen in their relationship and the ensuing conversation marks a real change for both of them. It is no longer Hillard exclusively needing Barton; the need is now mutual.

Their declaration of love is astoundingly honest. The two characters stand, facing one another; neither turns away; there is no embarrassment here, just an honest acceptance of the situation and of their love. This is a huge admission for both men - but perhaps more so for Hilliard. The fact that he has never declared feelings of love for *anyone* in his past, shows how crucial this moment is - not just to his character, but to the whole story, as it shows how much trust Hilliard now places in Barton. It is clear that for Hilliard to declare his love for anyone (whether male or female) is the greatest leap forward which his character has taken. The fact that his affections are directed towards another man is irrelevant. The love between these two men is realistic: they can see, know and understand each other's faults, but this does not change how they feel.

There would have been far-reaching consequences, at the time, of the discovery of this conversation, but this does not affect their statements of affection and the realisation and communication of their love seems to help Hilliard to relax a little. When the men are about to leave on the reconnaissance raid, Hilliard's sense of humour really shows through for the first time. He does not show as much fear of the forthcoming events as one might expect, although this may be because he is going too - this time Barton will not be alone and Hilliard can face anything, provided they are together. When they return from this raid, however, Hilliard is angry with Barton for the first time. He feels that Barton's inexperience is the reason behind the failure of the raid. However, when questioned by Captain Franklin, Hilliard makes no mention of Barton's possible mistake, so his anger may, in fact, be masking his own fears that he could have lost Barton as well as Coulter. This situation is reminiscent of an angry parent, who raves at a child for doing something dangerous, when actually, they are just pleased that the child is unharmed. Hilliard may also be hoping that, by becoming angry, he can teach Barton never to take such risks again. Either way, his rage soon passes and everything returns to normal.

The honesty which has developed between the two men makes it impossible for Hilliard to hide anything regarding the forthcoming attack. He would, ideally still like to protect Barton, but realises that it is more important to be truthful. During the night before the attack, the two men discuss their fears openly and, just like any other couple, Hilliard is keen to know whether he is the 'only one' for Barton or whether he has these feelings for anyone else. His 'joy' at finding that these sentiments are unique, leaves him unable to speak or to say any of the things which he would like.

The battle and its consequences mark yet another change for Hilliard, at least as far as practicalities are concerned. He is forced to face his worst fears: the loss of Barton being the greatest of all. The amputation of his leg seems remarkably insignificant to him, compared to facing life without Barton. He asks his mother to bring him copies of all the books which Barton had been reading, although he is unable to look at them when the arrive. He stares blankly out of the window, unwilling to focus on anything other than Barton, and wonders when he will be able to really live again. This depression is only lifted by the continued affection of Barton's family, whose correspondence brings him his only hope for the future.

In one of his unconscious dreams while he is lying wounded in No Man's Land, Hilliard imagines saying to Barton: 'I don't like myself much'. This is a revealing comment, showing how dissatisfied he had been with his life before meeting Barton. This earlier life had found him repressing his emotions, while always wondering if there there something he was missing, and waiting to feel more complete. It becomes obvious, as the novel progresses that Hilliard had, in fact, always been waiting for love.

Hilliard's role in the novel is to represent the typical Edwardian gentleman, who served in the First World War and to demonstrate how that conflict changed their lives. We are introduced to an upbringing which should, in theory, have prepared him admirably for the rigours and emotional hardships of warfare, by creating an intensely private and detached young man. Hillard, moreover, also shows us the exceptional nature of his generation. He feels the effects of the war and although he cannot always articulate his thoughts or feelings, because this does not coincide with his upbringing, he understands that the war will change everything - including himself. Through his love for Barton, he also learns to express himself better, to talk and become more tolerant, caring and thoughtful towards others. More importantly, however, he also learns to allow others the privilege of loving him, while accepting himself for the man he really is and for the man that he will become.

2. DAVID BARTON

David Barton is two or three years younger than John Hilliard (we are told in Part One that Barton is 'not quite twenty') and has just arrived in France for the first time. When we first meet him he is lively, with a warm and friendly personality. Barton is the antithesis of Hilliard: an optimist, always prepared to see the best in people, he has a talent for making others feel at ease and they instinctively like him, without necessarily knowing why. He is mature and wise for his years and those around him understand that he brings relief to their chaotic world, even though they barely know him. In short, people *need* him.

One of six children, Barton comes from a very close family. When he lived at home, his father, who is a doctor, had always encouraged David and his siblings to talk openly about their feelings: something which some of his new colleagues, especially Hilliard, initially find disconcerting. His letters home demonstrate this natural ability to reveal his thoughts: they are very frank and give vivid descriptions of trench life, his experiences and his feelings. Barton's letters contrast with Hilliard's correspondence which is cool and aloof, with little detail and no emotion.

He talks to Hilliard about his family, revealing details about their home life and individual personalities. He is completely comfortable with himself - even telling Hilliard that one of his brothers is a conscientious objector and that he had toyed with this idea himself before joining the army. This is not a normal admission for a serving soldier and shows that Barton's trust in Hilliard is instantaneous. He also encourages Hilliard, despite his obvious unwillingness, to talk about himself and his family. Even on the first evening together Hilliard finds that Barton has made him feel so relaxed that talking is not so 'difficult' as he would have imagined.

Barton sometimes finds Hilliard's reticence baffling. He is used to a large, somewhat boisterous and loving family and he considers this to be completely normal. He does not seem to have much experience of a more formal upbringing and he cannot understand the reserve of Hilliard's family, commenting in one of his letters to his own family, that they seem more willing to spend money than time on their son. Barton knows how much

Hilliard has come to appreciate hearing from his own family and feels disappointed on his friend's behalf, that the Hilliards cannot do likewise.

Although the attraction between the two men is almost immediate, Barton, it would seem, had initially been slightly in awe of Hilliard's reputation. He had heard the other men talking about him, knew that the Colonel held him in high esteem and knew that his name had been mentioned in dispatches. Barton had, like Hilliard, wondered whether he would really mind having his privacy invaded by a total stranger. Eventually, of course, all of these fears come to nothing and the two men become close, with Barton gently encouraging Hilliard to share details about himself.

Although Hilliard quickly becomes concerned for Barton's safety, Barton himself is more reckless. He is keen to be more involved in the war and craves excitement and adventure. This shows his youth and inexperience, which is what awakens Hilliard's fears, not only for his friend's physical safety, but also for the fact that Barton's personality may not survive the horrors of war. During the march to Feuvry, Barton soaks up the atmosphere and experience, observing the surroundings and the men. However, upon viewing the ruined town, he undergoes a change. Hilliard observes the expression on Barton's face and seems concerned that he is more affected by the sight of a ruined town than he had been by seeing a dead German pilot during the previous evening. Barton himself worries that his priorities seem to be becoming muddled.

Harris's death provides Barton with his first real experience of the war, at close quarters. When the problem with Harris first comes to light, Barton initially feels childishly annoyed that Hilliard automatically takes control of the situation in the cellar, even though he knows that it is not really his role. One senses, therefore, his feeling of pride when Hilliard returns and asks for help with Harris. This is then shattered when Harris is killed. Barton's reaction to this event is to feel useless and responsible - feelings which Hilliard is keen to dispel.

When Barton is chosen to go into the front line trenches to draw a map, he is initially pleased, not sensing any potential dangers. During his time in the front line, however, his viewpoint changes drastically. He witnesses many deaths and begins to wonder about the stupidity and futility of drawing maps, when men are dying. His recklessness comes to the fore and he stands up, placing himself in extreme danger for some considerable time. He does not think about Hilliard, or his family, or even himself. He simply cannot think of a single reason to be alive. Later, his return to Hilliard signifies another change in Barton's personality as, slowly but surely, the war begins to eat into him. He is losing his innocence and he really cannot see the point in continuing to participate in the war, if he cannot do some good. For the first time, Barton is reluctant to talk and the resultant tension between himself and Hilliard creates a deep sadness for both men.

Barton tries desperately to make sense of his experiences and to understand the incomprehensible. He is also worried that he will become callous and immune to the suffering of men. He really does not want to change, and yet he also appreciates that he must - or face suffering this acute sense of loss and deprivation every single time that someone dies. He wonders: 'What has happened to me?' Hilliard, as the more experienced soldier, helps Barton to realise that, simply by admitting to feeling and caring about each death, Barton will not be able become immune - as someone who did not care would show no concern, no sorrow, no sense of shame or guilt. Slowly, Barton begins to accept Hilliard's words.

The declaration of love which Barton makes shows how much he has come to trust and depend upon Hilliard. This statement carries a significant level of risk - especially given their circumstances and the consequences of their being discovered. However, Barton is prepared for this and demonstrates his belief in both Hilliard and their relationship by being the first to say what they are both thinking.

One soon senses that Hilliard has begun to replace Barton's family as a confidant - at least to some extent. He no longer shares every little detail of his life with them in his letters, as he has Hilliard to confide in now. Although he is obviously happy in his relationship with Hilliard, he still harbours feelings of guilt and a deep hatred of the war. He sympathises with the enemy soldiers who are in the same awful predicament as himself; he wants his family to understand how appalling the war is and how terrible are the conditions in which the men are forced to live. He also acknowledges that it is only really Hilliard who keeps him going, to the extent that he begins to wish that Hilliard had no family, so that he would not have to share him with anyone.

Hilliard's anger, following the unsuccessful and costly raid, seems to shock Barton. He is haunted by the fact that they have been forced to leave Coulter in No Man's Land, believing that he can hear him crying out from beyond the trenches. He tells his family that he has experienced nightmares about this experience, but that even he is disturbed by the fact that he has risked his life to safe a hedgehog, yet had been unable to do anything to help a dying man.

On the evening before the final attack, Barton's earlier excitement and longing for action have dissipated and been replaced by straightforward fear. Although he has not taken part in a proper attack, even his limited experiences have taught him to be afraid of the potential dangers which lie ahead. Just before the final attack, Barton and Hilliard talk openly about fear, life, the future and their love. This discussion dissolves Barton's fears and he is able to sleep. Early the next morning, the final words which Barton says to Hilliard are that he should 'never worry' about him again - an ominous statement which sends shivers of fear through Hilliard. He becomes worried that this may signify that something terrible is about to happen. With his terrors behind him, however, Barton regains some of his old composure: he helps those around him to come to terms with their anxieties, by admitting his own; he puts everyone else at ease. He is now excited about 'going over the top' for the first time, even though Hilliard's advice and his own experiences have given him a better understanding of how frightful it will probably be.

Barton's character is used to represent the effects of the war on an individual. As his experiences mount, he loses his perspective of the world. He cannot equate the war with his life at home and begins to wonder whether he will be able to recover mentally from these horrors, or whether they will have changed him forever. Susan Hill's portrayal of this character is well-drawn and effective. Through his words - both spoken and written - we learn that Barton is a kind, considerate, innocent young man, who makes and keeps friends easily but who is ill-equipped emotionally to deal with the effects of serving in the war. This is where Hilliard's character is allowed to be of benefit and both men eventually help each other, in different ways. Barton shows Hilliard that love - of every kind - is easy, if you just let it happen, while Hilliard helps Barton to understand his feelings about the war and to come to terms with the changes which are taking place within him. Barton does not survive, of course, but the reader is left with the impression that those whose lives he has touched are better, more fulfilled and happier people, just because they have known him.

3. COLONEL GARRETT

Colonel Garrett who, in civilian life, trained as a lawyer, has a wife and four daughters living on the south coast of England and is the most senior officer represented in the novel. Although we only meet him when Hilliard returns to France, we can see, through Hilliard's reactions to him, how much his earlier experiences of the war have affected his appearance and personality. However, we are also told that Hilliard remembers that, even before his injuries, Garrett had always seemed out of place in the trenches - resembling a city lawyer more than a serving officer. He is not an imaginative man, but is brave, steady, and extremely considerate towards his men.

It soon becomes clear that, in Hilliard's absence, Garrett has undergone a complete change of character. He has become an old man: his face is different; his cheeks are drawn in and his eyes are puffy. However, the changes in him are not just physical. Emotionally he seems to be shattered: it appears that the first weeks of the Battle of the Somme and what he witnessed during that time have altered Garrett beyond recognition. The only similarity between this Garrett and the one Hilliard used to know is his attitude towards his men. His air of calm has disappeared and in addition to this, he now drinks heavily. He has, essentially, lost his nerve. These changes are even more telling when Hilliard considers that Garrett had already seen considerable service in the war, prior to the beginning of the Battle of the Somme, so Hilliard realises immediately that the experiences of the battle must have been traumatic.

Garrett himself seems to feel responsible for some of the problems which he describes as having taken place during the battle. He has, however, been forced to keep his feelings to himself, as many of the more familiar officers, with whom he may have been able to share his thoughts, have been killed or wounded. We are, therefore, given to understand that Garrett has been 'waiting' for Hilliard's return, simply so that he may be allowed to unburden himself. While the battalion is resting behind the lines, he grows weary of doing nothing and the tension which builds up inside him adds to the air of depression and self-torture, which is only lifted once the men receive their orders to return to the front.

A shrewd man, Garrett demonstrates his understanding of the friendship between Barton and Hilliard, by inviting Hilliard to Headquarters while Barton goes into the front line to draw a map. Garrett knows that this will take Hilliard's mind off the situation. This episode shows him to a kind and considerate man, albeit somewhat unorthodox in his methods. He trusts Hilliard implicitly, speaking to him with great and unguarded sarcasm of the role of the Generals, which would not have been normal behaviour for a man in his position, especially when dealing with an officer whose rank is so junior to his own.

Eventually, his continued participation in the war breaks Garrett completely. He refuses to obey any further orders to send his men out on more pointless and costly raids. He takes his stand and is ordered to return to England in disgrace. It would seem that he is not entirely certain that he has taken the right action as he cannot bring himself to look any of his officers in the face when he reveals this information to them. There are two ways of looking at his position: it is a brave stand against the stupidity of continuing with these risky and fruitless raids; or he has simply had enough of war and wants to go home. Barton favours the former opinion, Hilliard the latter, explaining that the order to carry out more raids may have been just the excuse which Garrett had been seeking to precipitate his escape from the trenches. For Garrett, to be sent home, would have brought a great deal of shame upon himself and, possibly, his family. However, the destruction of his character has become so complete, that he does not seem to care about this: he would rather be thought of as a coward than have to stay in the war.

Despite their earlier friendship, when Garrett visits Hilliard in hospital, they find that they have 'nothing to say to one another'. Garrett, it would seem, has been able to return to his former life and this episode may show that perhaps the only real link between these two men had been the war - and their affection for Barton.

Garrett's character, like Barton's, demonstrates the psychological effects of participation in the war. His involvement has been more lengthy and he has had far more first-hand experience than Barton, and yet has managed to keep his head. However, The Battle of the Somme and its aftermath have proved too much for Garrett. The organised side of his personality seems affronted by the chaos which he witnessed in No Man's Land and this, coupled with the needless loss of life has brought about the significant changes to his personality. As such, he shows the reader how terrible the fighting really was: he had tolerated everything which came before, but this was too much.

4. CAPTAIN FRANKLIN

Franklin is the Adjutant of the battalion, which is a staff officer who helps his commanding officer with administrative affairs. He is a tall, efficient, detached man who is very self-controlled and calm in battle situations. He never becomes personally or emotionally attached to the men around him.

Hilliard seems to take an instant dislike to Franklin upon their first meeting, although this may be because Franklin is the only officer who does not respond well to Barton's stories during their first evening together. Rather than joining in with the others, Franklin sits in an aloof manner, not really seeming to focus on anything in particular, although the reader is given the impression that he is mentally noting everything which takes place.

He seems to seek to prevent Barton and Hilliard from becoming too close and from spending too much time together and this is something for which Hilliard also dislikes him. For example, Franklin suggests sending Barton on a gas course and he tells Hilliard that one of them must ride when they march to Feuvry, because there are insufficient horses for all of the officers. These may be perfectly logical and reasonable arguments, but Hilliard assumes that Franklin has also made these recommendations or orders so that he and Barton can spend less time together than they would like. Hilliard, unlike Barton, automatically assumes that Franklin has 'got it in for us'.

The reader gets a sense of frustration in the character of Franklin and his role in the war. At one point he sends for Hilliard because there has been some 'trouble over kit inspection', and we can see from this that his life is filled with comparative trivialities and that he possibly resents this. He is, however, well respected, because he keeps his head, even during a heavy bombardment. The men, therefore, trust him because they know they can rely on him, whatever happens.. Even Hilliard is forced to accept that as a soldier, Franklin is beyond reproach, even though he still does not like him as a man.

There could be many reasons why Franklin is portrayed as distrusting or disliking Barton and Hilliard. It may be that he understands the consequences of any close friendships which are formed in the trenches, in that if one party dies, the survivor can sometimes be less effective as a soldier.

This would be a concern for Franklin, who is doggedly efficient. Alternatively, he may sense that the relationship between Barton and Hilliard is more intense than the normal war-time friendships, which he would have seen before. Rather than interpreting this as straightforward homophobia (which would assume that Barton and Hilliards relationship is manifestly homosexual to the other characters), it would be more realistic to assume that he would be concerned for the morale of the men and the Battalion as a whole, should such a relationship come to light.

In the end, however, we see a more compassionate side to Franklin's character. He visits Hilliard in hospital, trying to ensure that the young lieutenant has everything he needs and seems genuinely concerned about the loss of Hilliard's leg and whether he will be able to cope. We also learn that he has written a compassionate letter to David's parents.

Through Franklin's character we can see the more 'routine' military perspective, both of the war and of the relationship which is forming between Barton and Hilliard. He is shown to be diligent and hardworking, but also brave and calm. He clearly distrusts Hilliard and Barton, worrying about their close contact and its implications, although one does not get the impression that he is malicious in his concerns.

5. CONSTANCE HILLIARD

Constance Hilliard is John's mother and despite the lack of outward affection
between the two, her influence is felt throughout the novel. She is beautiful,
poised, tall and elegant, paying particular attention to appearances - both her
own and those created by her family as a whole. She insists, for example, that
John should visit the Major, even though he is unwilling to do so. This is
because Constance feels it would be the 'right' thing to do, although she also
seems to show more sympathy for the Major than she does for her son.

The war does not really seem to affect her, but even if it did, of course the
reader would never know, because she would never show it. She 'does her
bit', organising local events for the war effort, but, again this appears to be
done from a sense of duty and status than any real concern for the soldiers -
it is what is expected of her by society, so she does it. Her dislike for allowing
personal feelings to interfere with duty is best demonstrated when she
comments on the poor appearance of the railway station, only mentioning in
passing that the station-master's son has been killed in action. She seems
disappointed that Kemble has allowed his standards to slip, yet makes no
allowance for his grief, showing that she has no tolerance for weakness.

Constance maintains that she regards John's return to the front in a similar
light to his earlier returns to boarding school when he had been a child. She
says that she has told herself not to worry about him and, if she has managed
to achieve this, she is a remarkably strong woman. Later, when John is
wounded, she seems more concerned with the practicalities of his recovery
than with how he feels. She wishes to be certain that he has everything he
wants in a material sense, rather than talking to him about what has
happened or how he will cope with the loss of his leg. She seems slightly
unnerved by John's comment that she looks 'beautiful'. He does not seem to
have ever told this to her before, and all she can do in return for his
compliment, is to 'smile'.

One can see, therefore, that it would be easy to judge Constance Hilliard as a
harsh, uncaring, selfish woman with no concern for anything other than her
own beauty and the way in which she and her family are perceived. However,
there are little hints that there is more to her than this. For example, when

John is about to go back to the front, she stands, looking out of the window, rather than directly at him. Perhaps this is because she cannot bring herself to watch his preparations for departure. It must be remembered that the character of Constance is a representative of the Victorian generation, probably trained from an early age to never show emotions. The situations with which she is now faced are difficult, so she deals with them according to her training.

One wonders whether she, like John, craves affection and attention. Her husband is clearly obsessed with his garden and at no time do we read of them spending any time together. Yet she seems keen that John should emulate his father - forcing him to attend dancing lessons as a child, for example. This may be because she has affectionate memories of her early days with John's father, and wishes for her son to be similarly happy. She seems to be an intensely lonely person and it could be that, in reality, she misses John terribly. She wants to accompany him to the station so that they may spend a little more time together before his departure. However, she still cannot break down her barriers sufficiently to wave goodbye.

Like many of her class and generation, Constance's character is forced to face up to the fact that war will bring about substantial and irreversible changes to her life. Despite her cold exterior, it would seem that even John has learned to appreciate that, under the circumstances, Constance is doing the best she can to show concern and affection for her son, and to adapt to the situation in which she has, unwillingly, found herself.

6. BETH HILLIARD

Beth is John's sister and is older than him by approximately eighteen months. In the novel, Beth serves several purposes. She represents John's youth and innocence; the time before the war, when they were best friends and he depended upon her for safety. In addition, Beth also shows us how life became during the war, for those left behind. John has gone to war and her character is shown to no longer have any real purpose.

At the beginning of the story, we learn through John's recollections, that he has a great dependency on Beth. In fact, at this stage, he probably looks upon her as more of a 'mother-figure' than his real mother. Beth helps him to overcome his fears and they share great bonds of friendship - almost like a little club of two people, linked by their mutual affection and the distance at which they are kept by their mother.

While he is convalescing from his injuries, John is haunted by his war-time experiences and is desperate to confide in Beth, in the hope that she will, as always, understand him and help him to come to terms with events. However, although he has only been away for a matter of months, he is surprised to discover how much she has changed. She is now more independent and the news that she is about to marry, signifies to him that she is 'gone completely' from his life.

Beth announces her intended engagement to John, stating that she is 'quite fond' of Henry Partington. Even John, whose life has been devoid of love, finds this description lacking in warmth or affection. However, Beth does not have that many options. She can either stay at home with her loveless family, or marry a much older man and hope that love will grow. There would have been very few young men left in the neighbourhood and Henry Partington is too old to have to go to war, which makes him a safe option.

Beth's letter to John announcing her marriage seems show her happiness in his eyes, but David Barton immediately doubts this, wondering if she feels 'anything at all'. This letter actually brings Barton and Hilliard closer together, in that Hilliard, for the first time, is prepared to share his family with Barton. In addition, however, Hilliard has also come to recognise how different his own life could have been. He becomes angry that Beth will have allowed herself to become just like their mother and says that he would rather be at the front and in danger, than sit through her wedding service, knowing exactly how her life will become. He resents the fact that Beth - of all people - has settled for something less than love. Of course, this only goes to show the reader how much Hilliard has changed. He has been fortunate enough to find love and he cannot accept that Beth will never really understand or experience these same feelings.

THEMES AND COMPARISONS

In this section I have looked in detail at some of the main themes of the novel *Strange Meeting*, paying close attention to how Susan Hill has portrayed them and how they impact on the reader's interpretation of the story. In addition, there is also some analysis on how other authors have dealt with similar topics in other literature of the First World War.

1. PORTRAYAL OF LOVE

'Things don't happen like this often in a lifetime.'

In her 'Afterword' Susan Hill states that the subject of *Strange Meeting* is not war - or the 'pity of war' - but 'human love'. In this novel, she introduces us to two men: one from a genteel, upper-class, unfeeling family; the other from a loving, demonstrative and happy background. They meet in an environment which might conventionally be thought of as 'loveless' - namely on the field of battle - and fall in love.

These central characters are both very different. Barton, the younger man, due to his close family upbringing, is good at expressing himself, making people feel at ease and relaxed in his company. Hilliard is restrained and aloof, having been trained never to show or express emotions of any type. Barton immediately draws Hilliard out of his shell, showing him that feeling comfortable with oneself, can enable anything. Hilliard's reaction to this is positive and almost instantaneous. He senses straight away that there is something very different about Barton, although, in common with many people who fall in love, he has absolutely no idea what this difference actually is. However, he does realise that he has been waiting for someone like Barton. He knows that there has always been something missing from his life and now he knows exactly what that is: love.

Anyone who has ever fallen in love will be able to appreciate that Susan Hill has skillfully captured this turbulent emotion. She conveys Hilliard's desperation to keep Barton safe; his jealousy when Barton is able to communicate with others, but not with him; his need to keep Barton to himself. To modern-day readers, these may all sound like possessive attributes, but the reader should bear in mind the context of the novel and that Hilliard is also aware that time may be extremely short for these two. He wants them to take every opportunity to spend their time together but is reluctant to plan for the future, believing that they should be satisfied with the here and now. Hilliard is also keen to keep enjoying the new sensations which his love for Barton have afforded him. His background, having been devoid of affection, makes him want to cling to his new-found love.

Barton and Hilliard find comfort in each other's company, in what is otherwise a harsh and unfriendly environment. They enjoy sharing their few pleasures, such as music, books, conversation and the contents of Hilliard's luxurious, if impractical, hampers. Above all, however, they share each other. Like most couples, they argue, they disagree on many topics, but none of this is shown to really matter. Anger or disappointment are soon forgotten, perhaps because time is so short for them that it seems pointless for them to dwell on the negative.

Their characters illustrate the depth of feeling and understanding which is possible between two people, regardless of their background or circumstances: that you cannot help who you fall in love with. The love which develops between them is intense and realistic, in that they know and accept each other's faults without these diminishing their affections. They care deeply about one another, desperately wanting and needing to survive and to be allowed to share their lives with this one person who has come to mean everything to them.

It must always be remembered that the fact that these 'lovers' are two men is completely irrelevant to the portrayal of their relationship and their affection.

This portrayal does, however, make *Strange Meeting* a somewhat unusual novel in this genre, in that many other authors of First World War literature have chosen to portray male relationships in the form of comradeship, hero-worship or just close friendship, reserving conventional 'love' for their heterosexual characters.

In *Birdsong*, for example, Sebastian Faulks shows us many different types of love. Firstly the tempestuous and ultimately disastrous affair between his central character, Stephen Wraysford and the wife of his French host, Isabelle Azaire. Secondly, the longer-lasting, less passionate love of Isabelle's sister, Jeanne Fourmentier, for Stephen, who, by the time they meet, has been emotionally damaged by the war as well as by his earlier affair. Finally, we see the love which Stephen feels for his comrade, Michael Weir, which only really surfaces after Weir's death. The love between these two men is completely different to the emotions portrayed in *Strange Meeting*. Weir and Wraysford do not declare their feelings for each other, although they both depend greatly on their friendship. Only after Weir's death does Stephen feel able to admit to himself how much he loves his friend, although now, of course, it is too late. A portrayal such as this is more commonplace in the literature of the First World War - it is still love, but it is not as intense or passionate as the feelings which Susan Hill shows us. Instead, Faulks gives an interpretation of the more usual feelings of shared hardships, comradeship and common understanding which existed quite naturally and genuinely between soldiers who were serving in the trenches. Sebastian Faulks also uses this relationship to demonstrate the journey which Stephen Wraysford has undertaken. At the beginning of the novel, he is a distant, enigmatic character, not easily affected by outside influences. His passionate affair with Isabelle changes his personality completely and, when she abandons him, he becomes even more withdrawn than before. War brings yet more changes as, with the help of Jeanne and Weir, Stephen learns to accept love from others and, eventually, to give it in return.

A different example can be seen in Pat Barker's *Regeneration*, where she portrays the real-life friendship between war poets, Wilfred Owen and Siegfried Sassoon. The two men meet in Craiglockhart Military Hospital and, partly through their shared interests in poetry, a strong friendship is quickly formed. Owen, it would seem, holds Sassoon in high esteem as both a poet and a soldier and their relationship could be said to take the form of hero-worship. Later in the novel, once Owen has left the hospital, Sassoon receives letters which make him wonder whether Owen has developed a deeper emotional bond than Sassoon had previously believed. The interesting point to note here is that as this relationship has its foundations in reality, it provides readers with a useful, realistic interpretation of how these friendships could be formed.

Novels which were written in the first half of the twentieth century often focus on male relationships similar to the one portrayed in *Birdsong* and for obvious reasons of censorship tend to portray these as comradely friendships. An example of this can be found in *All Quiet on the Western Front* by Erich Maria Remarque, where the central character, Paul Bäumer, is closely attached to many of his comrades, but particularly to one man: Stanislaus Katczinsky. Again, this is not a 'romantic' love, but an emotion born out of the war itself. Paul respects Kat, as he is known, but he also cares very deeply for him and when Kat dies, Paul feels that he has simply ceased to exist, saying: 'Then I know nothing more.' Thus, there is no doubting Paul's affection for Kat, but this relationship is not portrayed with the same level of closeness as the one between Hilliard and Barton.

As to the question of whether the relationship between Hilliard and Barton is a physical one - nothing could be less important, since the reader is not concerned with meaningless sexual romps, but with the development and fulfilment of real, honest love, which is about more than sex. This story is really about truth, trust and an unqualified acceptance of one's partner - whatever their gender.

However, readers should also bear in mind that the time of writing always affects the style and content of a novel, almost as much as the context of the story itself. As such, while homosexuality was legal for men over the age of 21 at the time this novel was written, this was a fairly new law. Until 1967, homosexuality was illegal in the United Kingdom, although obviously not unheard of. The fact that Susan Hill has chosen to portray her 'lovers' as men, but to leave out any graphic sexual content is, therefore, not surprising, especially given her desire to write about love, plus the time at which she was writing her novel and the context in which it is set. She takes the additional step however, of not even mentioning sex at all - there is no metaphorical 'closing of the bedroom door' in *Strange Meeting*. Nothing is left to the reader's imagination, because nothing happens. The portrayal of this intensity of emotion, without any physical contact between the two characters is beautifully achieved and, when other literature about this period is compared with this piece, one can see how exceptional the novel really is.

First World War novels which have been written in the last thirty years have tended to place a greater importance on sex than those written earlier and this is probably due to a more relaxed attitude towards sex generally, as well as the obvious problems relating to censorship and publication. Those authors who were writing in the first half of the twentieth century, especially, did not enjoy as much freedom as those who have been writing in the last twenty or thirty years. In *All Quiet on the Western Front*, for example, it is very clear that Paul and two of his comrades have a sexual liaison with three French women, while they are resting behind the lines. There is no salacious detail here, partly because of the aforementioned censorship issues, but also because Remarque wishes to point out how unsatisfying this encounter is for Paul. He says afterwards that he is 'not in the least happy', which is probably the opposite emotion to any which the reader may have expected and does not seem to mirror the feelings of his friends. This episode has, in fact, been used to show the deterioration of Paul's character as a whole. He has gradually come to believe that, even if he survives the war, he will never be able to live as he did before: that everything will be different for him and this sexual experience reinforces this belief, as he begins to wonder whether every aspect of his life - even sex - will always be tainted by the war

Birdsong by Sebastian Faulks, *A Long Long Way* by Sebastian Barry and *The Regeneration Trilogy* by Pat Barker - all novels written since 1990 - contain graphic sexual details. The two former novels feature heterosexual relationships in varying degrees of detail. This can, occasionally, feel contrived and a cynic might suppose that these scenes have been included to bolster sales, on the adage that 'sex sells'. Pat Barker's novels feature both heterosexual and homosexual liaisons, all of which include her central character, Billy Prior, a man who has been mentally and emotionally damaged by the war. *The Eye in The Door*, in particular, features vivid descriptions of an encounter between Prior and another officer, Charles Manning, which is used to demonstrate Prior's confused state of mind and his inability and unwillingness to behave in what would be considered a 'conventional' manner. The language in these scenes leaves nothing to the imagination, but the reader is also under no illusions as to Prior's emotional state.

So, why is *Strange Meeting* so exceptional? It is simply that, because the author has refrained from mentioning sex, she has avoided the trap of using it as a facile vehicle to graphically portray the love between her two central characters. She has managed to convey a mutually satisfying relationship between two people, who are happy to openly declare and discuss their feelings, rather than using sex as a metaphor for love. Of all the 'loving' relationships - sexual and otherwise - in First World War literature, this bond between Hilliard and Barton probably demonstrates the most realism and poignancy - because it is about love and because 'things don't happen like this often in a lifetime'.

2. THE EFFECTS OF WAR ON THE INDIVIDUAL

'What has happened to me?'

One of the main themes in much of the literature of the First World War is the effect on each individual character of their role and experiences in the conflict. *Strange Meeting* is no exception to this and, right from the beginning of the novel, we can see the impact which participation in the war has had on each of the people involved. Hilliard, although not perhaps as obviously affected as some of his comrades, clearly understands that something within him has changed. He feels like a stranger in his own home, unable to behave or react in the manner which is family expect. While he is convalescing at home, he also realises that the war has started to haunt him. During his stay in hospital, he had been unable to sleep, because of the interruptions and noises around him. At home, however, he does not want to sleep, because when he does he has disturbing dreams.

For Hilliard, however, things are further complicated by his desperate unhappiness, which is exacerbated by the feeling of not belonging anywhere. This leaves him only one option: to go back to the dangers of war, because at least there he fits in. Once he has boarded the boat to cross the Channel, Hilliard becomes much more relaxed. He knows exactly what he is returning to, and he accepts this.

Colonel Garrett, on the other hand, seems keen to escape the war completely. Whilst the reader is always given the impression that Garrett does not really belong at the front, during Hilliard's absence, matters have deteriorated and Garrett is now almost unrecognisable, when compared with the man whom Hilliard had left behind just weeks earlier. Although our first introduction to Garrett coincides with Hilliard's return to his unit, we know from Hilliard's reaction that he has undergone some severe trauma in the intervening time. His appearance has altered, he drinks heavily and seems nervous, all of which makes Hilliard wonder whether the Colonel can really be relied upon to lead the men. Garrett's explanation of events helps us to understand some of his torment, but his reaction is shown to be more extreme than any of the other characters. As the story progresses, Garrett's condition worsens further until, eventually, he is sent home for refusing to obey orders. He has seen too much death and waste to remain at the front. Whether he has deliberately chosen to disobey orders on a matter of principle, or whether this situation has simply provided him with an excuse to escape from the war, does not really matter, as either scenario shows how desperate he has become. He would rather face a possible charge of cowardice than remain in France any longer. The deterioration of his character is shown to us only through the reaction of Hilliard, although Barton also notices that Garrett 'looks very ill'. Garrett has been in the army for some considerable time, so his character is used to represent two elements of the effects of war - firstly the gradual breaking down of his personality over a period of prolonged service and secondly, his inability to cope, specifically, with the scenes he had witnessed during the Battle of the Somme. In this way, the author cleverly avoids having to fully describe these battle scenes - which are not really relevant to the telling of her story - by explaining their emotional, physical and psychological consequences instead.

The effects on Barton's character are even more extreme and noticeable to the reader, as we witness his deterioration first-hand, rather than retrospectively or through the eyes of another character. Barton changes from a lively, innocent, open and carefree young man at the beginning of the novel, into someone who, although still loving, has also become uncharacteristically cynical and angry. This is a gradual process, of which we only really witness the very beginnings and which has its roots in Barton's reaction when he first sees the ruins of the town of Feuvry. At this point he begins to question the war and its consequences, not just for those who die, but for those who must try to rebuild their lives afterwards. His fear becomes focused on life after the war. He is not afraid of dying himself but of how much he will change if he is continually exposed to death and destruction on this scale.

Barton clearly likes his life, his family and himself, although he is not conceited. He desperately wants his contented existence to remain the same and resents the changes which he feels he is undergoing. Harris's death marks the first of these, although Barton's feelings at this time are also tinged with guilt. It is his journey into the front line, when he witnesses many deaths, none of which serve any purpose whatsoever, that really alters his perspective. Following his return from this mission, he becomes uncommunicative - even sulky - and initially refuses any of Hilliard's offers of help. By the time of the final attack, however, their relationship has been repaired and Barton has come to realise that it is only Hilliard who really keeps him going.

The reader is able to understand Barton's feelings on two levels as they are seen in his letters home, which we know are an honest reflection of his thoughts, and also through the eyes of Hilliard. By explaining Hilliard's fears for his friend, Susan Hill enables the reader to experience a greater knowledge of how deeply affected Barton has become by these incidents. Hilliard's desperation that Barton should retain his innocence and remain unchanged shows how important this aspect is to both of these men. Barton cannot hide his real feelings from Hilliard for very long and the realisation that the war is beginning to enforce these changes awakens this genuine fear that they will not be able to live the same lives after the war, should they survive it.

The negative reactions to the experience of fighting in the First World War are portrayed, to a greater or lesser degree, in most of the literature of or about the period. These responses range from acute psychological reactions, such as those in Pat Barker's *Regeneration* or Rebecca West's *The Return of the Soldier*, to a transformation of the essence of a character, as shown in R. C. Sherriff's *Journey's End*. *Regeneration* features many cases of men who, either because they have been worn down, or because of a specific traumatic event, have become damaged by their experiences. One such incident refers to a man named Burns, who had been thrown into the air by a shell and had landed, face down in the decomposing stomach of a dead German soldier. As a result of this, he is unable to eat and vomits regularly. Other characters are not necessarily disturbed by one single event, but by the cumulative effects of continuous service. For example, Anderson, a surgeon, had operated successfully on wounded men for years, but suddenly, and for no apparent reason, he had become terrified of the sight of blood and, thus, was unable to continue in his profession.

Pat Barker makes a point, in many of the cases she portrays, of explaining the trauma or experiences behind the breakdown of each of her characters. Rebecca West does not choose to take this route. The central character in her novel *The Return of the Solder*, Chris Baldry, has suffered a complete breakdown, one of the symptoms of which is amnesia. Chris is unaware of his marriage to Kitty, the death of their infant son, or the war itself. Instead he believes himself to be still twenty-one years old and in a relationship with his first love, Margaret. His return home, in this condition, causes the three women in his life, Kitty, Margaret and Chris's cousin Jenny, to have to reach a difficult decision: should they allow him to remain in his imaginary world, safe from the war, or should they enlighten him and risk him having to return to the dangers of being a soldier. Rebecca West does not find it necessary to inform her readers of exactly why Chris has been so deeply traumatised, because her novel is not really about the war itself, but about the impact which it has on the four central characters and their relationships.

These two novels both portray this aspect of the war quite successfully. The reader is drawn into the lives of each of the characters and shown their suffering, not just through their own words, thoughts and actions, but also through the thoughts and reactions of those around them. This is not achieved with such a great degree of success in Sebastian Barry's *A Long Long Way*. Here, the author repeatedly tells us that his central character has 'changed', but nothing which Willie Dunne does or says actually encourages the reader to believe in this. We cannot perceive any real alteration in either his words, deeds or thoughts and simply being told that he feels he has changed is not really enough. Therefore, the effect of the war on Willie seems less realistic because it cannot be properly judged by the reader - either in the context of the novel, or with reference to other novels of the period.

A relatively simple narrative method for enabling the reader to see the change in an individual, rather than just be informed of it, is to demonstrate the alteration in one character, by showing us the reaction of another. Susan Hill achieves this in her description of the deterioration of Colonel Garrett, as seen through the eyes of Hilliard. R. C. Sherriff also uses this technique in his play, *Journey's End*. Here the audience is told at the very beginning that Stanhope's character drinks heavily and is soon made aware of the idea that he is war-weary and embittered. Raleigh, his friend from school, however, has no idea about Stanhope's war experiences and when the two meet, it is Raleigh's reaction to the alterations in his friend's personality which really enlighten the audience as to how much Stanhope has been affected by his prolonged participation in the conflict.

R. C. Sherriff has two distinct advantages over all of the other authors which have been mentioned, in that his piece is not a novel, but a play and that he had first-hand experience of the conflict himself. An audience watching his play is able to witness actors who can portray the effects of war by using expression and physical actions, rather than just reading words on a page, thus giving a more human and realistic element to this aspect of the performance.

Having a personal understanding of the effects of the war has helped both Sherriff and Erich Maria Remarque to portray this theme in their central characters. In *All Quiet on the Western Front*, Paul Bäumer reacts in a very similar way to David Barton. Paul is young, like Barton, and at the point where we meet him, still retains a certain amount of boyish innocence. Gradually, as the story progresses, his character is broken down, a deep depression sets in and Paul begins to wonder how he will ever be able to live a normal life again. The experiences of war have caused such a drastic change in his personality and outlook, that he cannot foresee a positive future at all. Sometimes it is his battle experiences that cause him to examine his feelings, but most of the time it is the reactions of his friends. For example, Albert Kropp, a former schoolfriend of Paul's reacts badly to being injured and then losing his leg. He tells Paul that he would rather die than be maimed. Initially, Paul cannot understand this attitude and worries that Albert will take his own life. It is the change in Albert's personality which makes Paul most concerned and he begins to brood on the idea that none of them will ever be the same again. We regularly see Paul wondering how he and his comrades can ever hope to return to a normal way of life after he war and whether life can ever be simply 'ordinary' again.

In Remarque's piece, however, there are two fundamental differences which give this aspect of the text more realism and significance than many of the others. Firstly, while he was writing this novel from first-hand experience, he had also become haunted by his own remembrances of the war and hoped that by telling this story he would be able to exorcise some of his demons relating to the conflict, in which he had served and been wounded. Secondly, he chose to write this piece in the first-person, thus making it more personal and giving the reader a feeling of a more direct involvement in the behaviour and thoughts of his central character. In a short preface to the novel,

Remarque comments that it is not his intention to accuse or confess and that he is not writing the story as though war was a form of adventure. Instead he says that he will 'try simply to tell of a generation of men who, even though they may have escaped its shells, were destroyed by war', because for many who fought in the conflict and survived, that remained their overriding impression of what war does to men.

3. THE HOME FRONT

'She knew nothing about him now.'

Another popular theme in fictional portrayals of the First World War, this aspect is given a reasonable amount of attention in *Strange Meeting*. The novel actually starts on the home front, with Hilliard recovering at home from his wounds. This part of the story is told, exclusively, from Hilliard's perspective and the reader is immediately made aware of how uncomfortable and out-of-place he feels. He finds the attitude of civilians intolerable; he argues 'bitterly' with his father; he is dismayed by the Major's continued references to the usefulness of the cavalry in battle; he marvels that life seems to go on just as though there were no war.

Hilliard's mother, Constance, seems determined that the war should have as little direct impact as possible on her own life. She and her friends gather and drink tea while they knit socks and mittens for the soldiers, but this has a feeling of make-believe, as far as John is concerned. The world of his home-life has become alien to him, making a return to the front seem positively appealing. He also becomes angry with civilians who believe that they understand the war - that they 'know'. However, following his arguments with his father, Hilliard chooses to remain 'silent', as though he realises that nothing which he says can change the viewpoint of someone who refuses to listen to reality.

The feeling which the reader receives, that those on the home front are unsympathetic and unworthy, is intensified by the fact that the civilian characters at the beginning of novel are, generally speaking, given unfavourable characteristics. The Major, for instance, is opinionated and selfish, more concerned with the welfare of himself and his dog, than with anything which is happening in the war. In addition, he believes that he understands the conflict better than Hilliard, simply because he was once a soldier himself. In contrast, the soldiers at the front are shown to be helpful and affable. Hilliard recalls instances where the men had helped and supported each other. This contrast in the characteristics of the two types of people makes the reader less inclined to like or sympathise with the civilians and therefore, more tempted to disregard their opinions.

This is a fairly common device and is coupled with a popular portrayal of the home front - namely that civilians are often shown to be complacent, callous and uncaring towards the men at the front. However, Susan Hill also contrasts this stereotypical depiction by showing us the behaviour of Barton's family, who are full of understanding and compassion, rather than opinionated and insensitive. David Barton writes long, honest and heartfelt letters to his family, keeping back none of the horrific details about the war, revealing not only how awful everything is, but also how it makes him feel. Due to the fact that this family have an open relationship with David, they respond sympathetically. Their compassion then extends to Hilliard, as David's friend. So, in fact, while Susan Hill has provided the reader with two contrasting views of the civilian perspective, these are as much a reflection of the families and characters themselves, as they are of the home front in general.

Many other novelists portray the home front in a more one-sided and stereotypical style. Sebastian Faulks, in *Birdsong*, gives us two separate occasions when the home front attitude could be analysed. In both cases, however, he presents us with a similar picture. Michael Weir visits England on leave and experiences a situation similar to that of John Hilliard. His father is not interested in listening to Weir, believing that the newspaper reports which he reads give him all the information he requires. Weir, like Hilliard, comes from a well-to-do background and his parents have never been very interested in him, so this representation is of less value than it might otherwise have been, as it tells us more about Weir's character, than it does about the life of civilians at the time.

Stephen Wraysford views the home front in a different way from most other characters, in that although he is English, he has no connections, family or home to return to, being as he has not lived in England since 1910. He, therefore, has a more objective viewpoint of the civilians he meets, whom he finds to be complacent, arrogant and even resentful of him. Stephen has no personal motives for disliking the people he meets, so the reader could interpret these reactions as being a more accurate portrayal.

A similar perspective is portrayed in *All Quiet on the Western Front*, where Paul Bäumer returns home on leave. The male civilians are shown to be arrogant and opinionated - even Paul's father is keen to show him off in uniform to all of his friends. Again, just as in *Birdsong*, these men believe the newspaper reports and deride Paul's viewpoint, because he cannot see the 'bigger picture' as they can. However, although this may seem just as clichéd as the portrayals given by Sebastian Faulks, there is one major difference, which gives Remarque's piece a greater sense of balance. Paul's mother and sister are shown to be sympathetic and concerned for him. They are not just worried about how much he is suffering at the front, but also about simple practicalities, such as that he has enough to eat, despite the food shortages which they are experiencing at home. The purpose of these portrayals within the context of this novel is to show the reader how disconnected Paul has become because of the war. He finds no comfort at home at all - not even with his mother - and, like Hilliard in *Strange Meeting*, eventually just longs to return to his comrades, where he can feel more 'at home'.

Home front arrogance and complacency are taken to another level in *Not So Quiet...*, by Helen Zenna Smith. Here, the central character, Smithy, serves as an ambulance driver just behind the front lines, in a job which involves witnessing some of the worst injuries and living in constant danger of being killed. These hardships, coupled with the death of her closest friend, eventually lead Smithy to have a breakdown and she returns home. All through her time at the front, however, the reader has been made aware that Smithy's mother and her friends regard their own sacrifices as being of greater importance than anything else. Mrs Smith sends her daughter long letters about her committees, boasts frequently about how many young men she has managed to recruit to the 'cause' and moans about how much additional work she has to do herself.

Once back at home, Smithy renews her acquaintance with Roy Evans-Mawnington, the son of a family friend, who is at home on leave. The couple become engaged just before Roy returns to the front, where he is seriously wounded. Smithy's mother is quick to write to Smithy and urge her to 'do her duty' and not cancel the wedding. She also hopes that Roy's suffering will teach the 'cowards' a lesson. Although this representation may seem extreme today, it was not uncommon at the time, especially - although not exclusively - among the upper classes, who are represented in this novel. For many, life was about doing one's duty and being seen to do the right thing.

Regeneration and *The Return of the Soldier* are different novels altogether, in that they are set entirely in England. This makes the contrast between life at the front and life at home more difficult to achieve. Rather than the reader being able to see the difference, we have to understand it from the reactions of the characters involved. In *Regeneration*, for example, Billy Prior becomes extremely angry at his perception of the arrogance of the people at home, who carry on as though the war did not exist. He wants to make someone suffer, physically, for the complacency which he witnesses. This extreme reaction enables the reader to understand how enraged soldiers might become, when their suffering - especially the mental anguish of someone such as Billy Prior - seemed to count for so little.

The Return of the Soldier offers us yet another treatment of this topic. Here, again, the novel is set entirely on the home front, but on this occasion there is no mention of the details of the war at all. We are not told why Chris Baldry, the central character, has become so traumatised; we have no idea what he has experienced while participating in the conflict. However, the reader still receives the impression that the home front was - at least in part - filled with uncaring and arrogant civilians. This is achieved simply by the creation of one character: Kitty Baldry. Kitty is Chris's wife, although, due to his amnesia, he knows nothing about her and believes himself to be still in a relationship with his first love, Margaret. As such, the reader might expect to feel sympathetic towards Kitty since, through no fault of her own, she seems to have effectively lost her husband. However, Rebecca West makes sympathy for Kitty impossible by creating her as her a vain, selfish, arrogant woman, whose sole concern is that nothing whatsoever should be allowed to interfere with her own personal happiness.

The reader's distaste for Kitty is, however, balanced by the establishment of two further characters: Chris's cousin, Jenny and his first love, Margaret. For these two women, their prime concern is Chris and his future. They are both worried that, by returning him to reality, he will be forced back into the war and will have the face the danger of service in the front line. In addition, in his fictitious world, Chris is unaware this his young son is dead and, both women fear his reaction to rediscovering this dreadful fact. Rebecca West has provided two different perspectives of home front attitudes, which could not be more different. In addition this portrayal is also a negative reflection of the class system, in that Kitty is seen to be a spoiled, childish snob, while Margaret, although described as physically unattractive and dowdy, is shown to have far kinder qualities than her upper-class counterpart.

4. HOPE

'When would it begin?'

Strange Meeting is an unusually hopeful novel in this genre, which is surprising, given that, in common with many other books, the plot involves the death of one of its central characters and the mutilation of another. Upon completing the novel the reader is left with an uplifting sense that, regardless of all the hardships and suffering which have been meted out to John Hilliard, he has survived and will continue to grow in the future. Hilliard has, after all, lost just about everything and all of his worst fears have been realised. His family, who were already distant before the war, are even more absent from his life, for the simple reason that they no longer understand him at all. He is, however, resigned to this situation, as he knows that they will never change. His leg has been amputated, making his future very uncertain indeed. Worst of all, however, his beloved David has been killed. Hilliard's sense of isolation is compounded by the fact that nobody really knows what happened to Barton and Hilliard understands that he will forever be one of the 'missing'. Despite all of this, the novel ends on a optimistic note, with Hilliard looking up and towards the future.

It is made clear to the reader that any optimism of which Hilliard is capable, is only the result of Barton's love and the continued attentions from his family. Without these there would have been no hope for Hilliard. While recovering in hospital, he sits and wonders when his life will begin again, when he will stop waiting for it to start, and be able to realise that it already has. Despite the sense of depression and sadness here, there is also an underlying hope, because at least Hilliard knows that his life *will* start again. So he does not ask himself 'if', but 'when' his existence will have more meaning and when he will return to something resembling normality.

The journey to Barton's home, therefore, signifies the beginning for Hilliard, rather than the end, as only the Bartons can provide him with the support he really needs. This, the reader senses, will come not just in the form of physical and emotional comfort, but also by connecting him to the only thing of any significance: his memories of David.

Many other authors have chosen to show us a view of the First World War in which hope has been abandoned. The difference between most of these and *Strange Meeting* is that here we are merely offered a snapshot of the war and it only provides us with a background for the main focus of the story, which is the relationship between Barton and Hilliard. As such, the war is never really allowed to dominate the story. The characters spend approximately three months at the front and not all of that is spent in the trenches. One wonders whether Hilliard would have been shown as so hopeful had he remained a little longer in France after Barton's death, rather than being maimed in the same battle.

A great number of other novelists have chosen to describe more of the conflict itself, giving greater emphasis to the battles and their effects, than Susan Hill has. In the case of *A Long Long Way* by Sebastian Barry, this has the adverse effect of there simply being too much war. So many things happen to the central character that it would be impossible for the reader to believe in him retaining any semblance of hope for the future. Not only does he take part in almost every major battle of the First World War, he is wounded, shell-shocked and sees most of his comrades die. In addition, his girlfriend abandons him and his father disowns him. Hope, in such circumstances, simply has no place. Therefore, the novel has a depressing tone, which would normally be overcome by the foundation of strong, realistic friendships, which are sadly missing from this story.

In *Birdsong*, Sebastian Faulks also looks at the war in a greater degree of detail than Susan Hill, although we only join the conflict in 1916 at the beginning of the second part of the novel. The author then dips into the war throughout the story, returning to it in 1917 and 1918. As such, rather than perceiving this as a never-ending, relentless process, as in *A Long Long Way*, the reader is offered some relief. Again, a great deal happens to the central character, Stephen Wraysford. He is firstly abandoned by his married lover, then he is wounded several times, left for dead and then discovered purely by accident; his greatest friend is killed, following an argument between the two men and finally, he is buried underground and rescued by a German soldier, whose brother he has recently killed. In this instance, however, hope seems to be a more fitting emotion for the central character to experience. This is because Stephen Wraysford begins the novel in a state of despair when his lover leaves him and he becomes cut off from everything around him. During the war, he slowly learns to love again and it is this which, even when he is entombed and can see no chance of survival, allows him to begin to hope. In addition, the format employed by Sebastian Faulks enables the reader a greater level of understanding that life does go on. He introduces a 'modern' section, in which Stephen's granddaughter, Elizabeth Benson, sets about tracing her ancestry. Although the ending is a little clichéd and convenient (Elizabeth becomes pregnant and gives birth to a son, thus enabling her to fulfil a promise which Stephen had made to one of his comrades during the war), the reader cannot help but understand that, even out of the greatest adversity, it is always possible to hope.

All Quiet on the Western Front gives yet another perspective, in that Remarque's central character, Paul Bäumer gradually loses heart as the story progresses. His friends are nearly all killed or wounded and he can see little hope for the future. However, just at the end of the novel, Paul begins to feel stronger; he remains unsure as how how he will cope in the future and what it will hold for him, but he feels strong enough to at least begin to contemplate it. In this way, Remarque builds up the reader's expectations, encouraging us to believe that Paul will survive and eventually learn to live a normal life again. Then, in a footnote, Remarque tells us that, in fact, Paul died. The reader might expect to feel slightly disappointed, or cheated by this ending and yet it is handled with such care, that even Paul's death does not detract from the reader's sense of fulfilment upon finishing the novel. We learn that, upon his death, Paul's expression had been one of calm gratitude, implying that he had actually been relieved to die. This may seem like a depressing ending, except when one recalls the philosophy which Barton and Hilliard had been discussing in Strange Meeting: namely, is it easier to die than to live, knowing that the quality of one's life will always be diminished? Paul Baümer also seems to have been asking himself this question at various times in All Quiet on the Western Front, wondering how he could possibly hope to return to his old home and his life, which could never be the same as it had been before the war.

Returning, finally, to Strange Meeting, one could remark that it would be easy for Hilliard to give up. It would have been reasonably in character for Susan Hill to portray him as taking his own life, or simply as adopting an 'existence' at his parent's house, seeing out his days in a world where everyone he cares about has gone forever and everything has changed beyond recognition. Equally, she would not have been straying too far from realism to have killed both her central characters in that one battle. However, she has not chosen that route. Instead she has given us a realistic portrayal of one man's reaction by showing him, like so many others of a generation to whom Susan Hill had wished to pay tribute, taking the bravest decision of all in the circumstances: to live and try to begin again.

CRITICAL ANALYSIS

1. INCONSISTENCIES

Although *Strange Meeting* is, in my opinion, probably one of the best novels in this genre, it does contain a few minor, but niggling, inconsistencies. These are fairly slight, but nonetheless distracting:

A. THE AGES OF THE CHARACTERS

In Part One we are told that in April 1916, when he had gone out to France, John Hilliard was 22 years old, and this information is confirmed by the statement:
'John George Glover Hilliard, Born 10 April 1894...'
So, when Hilliard returns to France in August 1916, he would still be 22 years old.

We are then told that Barton is 'not quite twenty', which implies that when he and Hilliard meet he is 19 years old.

Later, when we are told how Barton had first feared meeting Hilliard, we are informed that Hilliard is 'only a year older' than Barton.

B. BARTON'S FAMILY

When Hilliard and Barton first become acquainted, Barton explains that he is one of six children: 'Three brothers older than me, two sisters, younger.'

Later, we are told that Barton had previously gone on a walking holiday with his *younger* brother.

In addition, when Barton goes to talk to Harris in the cellar of the house in Feuvry, he reminds himself that Harris is the same age as his youngest brother, Edward, who is two years younger than David Barton. As such both Edward and Harris would only be 17 years old.

David's brother Edward, we have already been told, is in prison because he is a conscientious objector. However, if Edward is only 17 years old, he would be too young be conscripted anyway. And, while men - or boys - tried throughout the war to enlist voluntarily under the legal age limit of 18 (19 for overseas service), it would hardly seem realistic to have a conscientious objector taking this course of action.

C. BATTLES

To the best of my knowledge, the place names (such as Feuvry, Barmelle Wood, Percelle etc) which Susan Hill has used, are fictitious. This is probably a good decision on the part of an author as it saves them having to be historically or geographically accurate. However, when Hilliard and Coulter are discussing Coulter's 'feeling' that something is about to happen to the men, Hilliard recalls a soldier with whom he had been acquainted before his injury. This man, Armstrong, had written a letter and been desperate to ensure that, should anything happen to him, Hilliard would see it safely delivered. Armstrong had had a premonition - or at least a 'feeling' - that on the day in question, he would be killed. Hilliard, at the time, had been incredulous, since Armstrong had been extraordinarily lucky throughout his time in France. He recalls that Armstrong had been with Colonel Garrett since the beginning and had seen action at 'Ypres, Loos, and then the whole of the Somme', without once being wounded.

Herein lies the problem: Hilliard had been injured in the second week of July and he is recalling this incident as having taken place *before* his injury. The Battle of the Somme began on 1st July 1916 and continued until November of the same year. Therefore, being as Armstrong must have been killed in the first days of the Somme, he could not possibly has seen action throughout the 'whole' of it.

None of these inconsistencies really detract in any way from the telling, or enjoyment of the story, and many people fail to even notice them. Susan Hill's stated wish was to tell us a story about the people who fought in the conflict, rather than about the conflict itself and this she has achieved. However, her editor should have picked up on these minor problems and seen to it that they were corrected.

2. NARRATIVE STYLE

Strange Meeting is written in the third person, by an all-seeing or omniscient narrator. This form makes it quite difficult for the author to reveal the thoughts of all of the characters involved. The story is, therefore, told predominantly from the perspective of John Hilliard. Much of the information we glean is through his thoughts or reactions to people or events. The opinions of David Barton are mainly revealed by the use conversation and lengthy letters, written to his family. Other characters, such as Colonel Garrett and Coulter, are revealed to us through their own words and by the conversations and reactions of the people who surround them. Captain Franklin, on the other hand, remains somewhat of an enigma, because he rarely talks. However, we are always aware that Hilliard does not like him.

The creation of characters in novels, especially ones which are as personal as *Strange Meeting*, can sometimes be said to suffer from being written from the perspective of a narrator, rather than one particular personality, in the first person. This is because it can be more difficult for the reader to become truly familiar with the main characters and also because the novel, therefore, sometimes lacks a realistic, individual quality. On the other hand, novels which are written in the first person can sometimes be too one-sided, and fail to show the reader more than one viewpoint. Whichever choice an author makes it is up to them to convey each character's thoughts in a coherent fashion, without allowing this to become clumsy or contrived, while remaining, at all times, within the personality of the character(s) involved.

Susan Hill has achieved all of this very well. As the main character, Hilliard's reactions and thoughts are believable and realistic because the author has taken the time to build his up his personality in the first part of the novel. This enables the reader to interpret his actions more easily, so we comprehend, for example, how angry he feels that he will have to share his billet with a new officer. Later, Susan Hill goes on to reveal even more about Hilliard through the reactions of the people around him. So, we learn that Hilliard is a well-respected officer, not by being told this in so many words, but because the other officers are genuinely pleased to see him upon his return and because we are informed that Colonel Garrett has been 'waiting' anxiously for him to come back to the front.

Similarly, with David Barton, rather than a clumsy explanation of his characteristics, the reader discovers him at the same time and pace as Hilliard himself. His personality is gradually explained, through conversation, reaction and, especially, his letters home. This is made easier by the fact that Barton has been created as an 'open' character, who naturally reveals his innermost thoughts, with disarming honesty. Therefore, we can see Barton's reactions to various experiences by the tone of his letters. His early correspondence seems to be full of wonder and excitement, but as time progresses and he sees more of the conflict, the nature and style of his letters changes. His absolute frankness with his family permits him to reveal his state of mind, in a manner which the reader finds easily accessible. This is not clumsily displayed, but seems to be this character's natural reaction to his new circumstances.

Outside of the creation and reinforcement of characters, there is also a secondary use for Barton's letters, in that they disclose various aspects of the plot. So, for example, we learn different details, such as who has died, whether the Company has moved, what type of accommodation they are in, whether they anticipate seeing action soon. In this way, the reader is almost subliminally informed of the events which have taken, or are about to take place. This is a subtle and natural use of letters as a narrative tool. Orders and reports are used to similar effect, as we learn, for example, of the fact that nine men died in the blast at Feuvry, not through a contrived, forced conversation, but in a footnote to Colonel Garrett's report to Headquarters. Such devices are used to great effect as, not only do we learn more detail about this event, but also the fact that Garrett had taken this opportunity to suggest that Feuvry is 'unsuitable for billeting purposes'. This tells us, in a very subtle manner, that Garrett is concerned for the welfare of his men, rather than blindly obeying orders, which had been written, we discover more than a year earlier. Thus, in these two short excerpts, we are told details about the events at Feuvry, given an insight into Garrett's personality and told something about army procedures. This could, naturally, all have been achieved in a conversation, or a series of conversations, but to do so would probably have felt artificial and out of character.

Much of the language used in *Strange Meeting* is understated and concise. There are no lengthy, gory descriptions of battles or death. Most of the detail in these instances is left to the reader's imagination. So, when Susan Hill tells us that on board the boat, when returning to France, Hilliard realises that it is 'easy to pick out the ones who had been here before...', there is no need to embellish upon this statement. The reader already knows how tired and war-weary Hilliard has become and how, although he looks forward to returning to France, there is also a great feeling of trepidation within him, because he knows exactly what to expect. The new recruits would not have shared these fears, but we do not need to have this explained to us in so many words, because it is obvious.

Where there are descriptions of battle, wounds or death, these are effective but subtle. In Hilliard's nightmares, he remembers 'bodies piled on top of one another in layers, like sandbags, making a wall'. Later, Barton recalls how he 'had watched stretcher parties scrape and shovel up what was left of half a dozen men...' In each case there is no further explanation. There is no lengthy description of exactly what is involved, how the people involved might feel, what they can smell, and so on. No such clarification is required, because the reader can use their imagination. This is one of the greatest successes of this novel, in that Susan Hill gives her readers credit for having sufficient intelligence and vision to conjure these images, without having to run to vast, wordy and unnecessary explanations.

Although Susan Hill is not graphic or vivid in her descriptions of death or wounds, we can still learn how devastating the effects of such events have been, by observing the reactions of the characters involved. So, Hilliard's response to his nightmarish vision of piled up bodies, is to cry out: 'Jesus God, help me...'. This desperate plea for help makes further explanation superfluous.

There are a couple of points in the story which do feel slightly strained in their creation. For example, we are told quite early in the novel, that Hilliard's great fear is the loss of a limb: 'the loss of a part of himself'. This nightmare then becomes a reality when Hilliard's leg is amputated, but at the time when this actually happens, Hilliard barely seems to notice. Barton's death absorbs him to such an extent that this long-dreaded maiming becomes of secondary importance. In this way, Susan Hill is demonstrating the depth of Hilliard's love for Barton, by explaining that nothing else really matters to him. Equally, in one of Barton's letters, he tells his family about Sergeant Locke, whom he paints as a great father-figure to the men and whom they love 'because he is so straight and conscientious'. Later, in the same letter, Barton tells his parents that this man has been killed. We have been informed that he has five sons at home and that he was, essentially, a simple fisherman. To have this character introduced, discussed in such detail and so warmly, and then immediately killed, is a rather ruthless and contrived means of reinforcing the idea that life in the trenches is extremely transient.

The creation of atmosphere is vital in novels about the First World War. If this is not done successfully, the story loses a great deal of its realism. In reality, one of the many features of service during the conflict was the element of boredom. Most of a soldier's time was spent in preparation, or waiting for attacks to take place, rather than participating in battles. As such, the creation of a sense of frustration and anticipation is important, but this is not always successfully achieved. In *Strange Meeting*, one of the main reasons for the failure of this, is that Hilliard and Barton are just too contented in each other's company. Barton is shown to be impatient and anxious to experience everything which war has to offer, but there is not a really convincing atmosphere of boredom.

In creating a feeling of tension between the two central personalities, however, the author has achieved a much greater degree of success. When Barton becomes withdrawn, the reader can easily sense and understand Hilliard's frustration at being unable to help his friend. The atmosphere between the two men is brilliantly created, as is the desperate feeling of sadness when they are unable to communicate. Hilliard is desolate that he cannot find the words to express himself. He wants to explain to Barton how important their friendship has become and also that Barton's reactions to his experiences of the war are normal and acceptable.

This novel has a very subdued, quiet atmosphere; it moves slowly, allowing the reader to learn about the individual characters and their experiences in a steady, unhurried manner. In addition - and perhaps unusually for a First World War novel - there is not too much focus on the conflict itself, as the author has chosen instead to concentrate on the people concerned. The reader is given sufficient information to understand the setting and context of the novel, without being overwhelmed by military details. The conflict is already two years old at the time the novel is set, but the innocence of Barton's character allows there to be a mood of discovery, and even wonder, underpinning the story. Both of the central characters are taken on a journey and are awakening to new aspects of their lives. In Barton's case, the war forces him to grow up and see the world in a harsher, but perhaps more realistic light. Hilliard, on the other hand, is discovering the power of his heretofore hidden emotions, by learning to love and to be loved. It is due to the author's emphasis on the creation of her characters and their place that this novel works as well as it does and, despite its minor flaws, remains one of the finest.

COURSEWORK ASSISTANCE

The coursework element of A-Level study involves the student reading, understanding and interpreting their chosen text; analysing the way in which the writer has used structure, form and language to achieve their purpose; comparing or connecting it to other texts within this genre and demonstrating an understanding of the context in which the novel has been set. In this section I have attempted to provide some assistance for students who are using *Strange Meeting* as part of their coursework. In the first section, I provide some suggestions for essay titles and content for the prose element of coursework studies. In the second section, I will look at using *Strange Meeting* in comparison with some of the plays of the First World War.

1. ESSAY SUGGESTIONS

PERSONAL INFORMED INTERPRETATION

Students who decide to write this type of essay should be aware of what is meant by the term 'personal informed interpretation'. If you are struggling to understand this, think of the phrase as three separate words:

'Personal' - What does the novel mean to *you*? How does it make *you* feel? This does not have to be a positive feeling - just because someone you know loves this novel above all others, does not mean that you have to! However, do not just write your essay in the form of a 'rant' - your reasons, whether you love or loathe the novel, must be reasoned and reasonable, but above all, personal.

'Informed' - Your essay must demonstrate that you have understood the novel. In addition, you will be required to endorse this understanding with wider, relevant reading, showing that you have selected and studied appropriate texts in order to support your arguments. In other words, you must show that you are making 'informed' judgements.

'Interpretation' - You need to explain your understanding of the text. In other words, you cannot just write 'When Susan Hill says 'He felt a moment of singing happiness', she is informing the reader that Hilliard is pleased to be returning to the war.', and leave it at that. You must go on to explore Hilliard's feelings for his family and compare these with his sense of belonging in the army; explain Susan Hill's use of the word 'singing' in this context - Hilliard is clearly more than just cheerful. You must explain, using the text, why Hilliard feels isolated and how army life allows him to remain thus. So, whatever topic you have chosen to discuss or explore in your essay, you should show that you have thought about the subject in hand and reasoned through your explanations, reinforcing these with highly relevant and specific references to the text.

Strange Meeting lends itself to many essays, focusing particularly on themes, characters, and language. Students need to choose a task with which they feel comfortable and which enables them to answer all of the assessment objectives required, concisely and accurately, demonstrating that they have understood the text. The following are just a few suggestions for possible essay titles and content, together with ideas for specific further reading:

(a) 'Explore the portrayal of love in *Strange Meeting*.'

- Here, there are two possible choices. You could either focus on the love between the two central characters, or you could compare their relationships with their families, focusing on how their contrasting upbringings have influenced their characters.

- If choosing to examine the relationship between Barton and Hilliard, you should explore how Susan Hill has portrayed their love. Focus on the differences in their characters and how these are overcome. Also pay particular attention to their conversations and show that their growing knowledge of each other forms the basis of their relationship. You could discuss how their relationship is different to those of other soldiers.

- You may choose, within this topic, to examine the extent of their relationship. Susan Hill states in her 'Afterword' that she did not 'intend the conclusion to be drawn' that the two men have a physical relationship. The fact that so many people, evidently, ask this question of the author, implies that, for some, this aspect is of importance to their interpretation of the novel. Do you, therefore, feel that the novel would have worked better had this element been made clear or do you (like me), feel that this is completely irrelevant?

- If you decide to focus on the upbringing of these two characters and the ways in which the two families show - or don't show - love, you should pay particular attention to the letters which are sent by Hilliard and Barton, and those which each man receives. Also look at how the families influence each of the men and their outlook on relationships.

- Other novels which would help to contrast with the relationship between Hilliard and Barton might include *All Quiet on the Western Front* (Erich Maria Remarque) and *Birdsong* (Sebastian Faulks). Although the male friendships which are featured in these are different from the one in *Strange Meeting*, they do help to see the different way in which Susan Hill has chosen to portray her characters and their feelings. If looking at the attitude of the families, you could try reading *Not So Quiet…* (Helen Zenna Smith), which again provides a useful contrast.

- Close relationships between men in the trenches were fairly standard. For two officers to express a romantic love for each other was not, however, commonplace. A good study of this topic can be found in the poetry anthology entitled *Lads - Love Poetry of the Trenches*, edited by Martin Taylor.

Additional information and guidance on this topic, both in *Strange Meeting* and other novels, can be found in this Study Guide, in the Chapter entitled *Themes and Comparisons - Portrayal of Love*.

(b) 'Explore the portrayal of the home front in *Strange Meeting*.'

- When looking at this topic, students should pay attention to all the aspects of the home front which are portrayed in Strange Meeting. Hilliard's visit to the Major and to London should be given emphasis, as they demonstrate the attitudes, not of the character's family, but of ex-soldiers and the general population.

- The Barton family seem to have a different perspective on the war when compared to the Hilliards. The letters which they send are very different and should be examined closely.

- Focus also on the reaction of Hilliard to the attitude at home. He seems angry and resigned at the same time (notice, for example, that he argued 'bitterly' with his father and then 'stayed silent').

- Examine Hilliard's thoughts regarding how Colonel Garrett might react to being at home again.

- Many novels also portray the home front, usually in an unfavourable light, focusing on depicting the callous lack of understanding displayed by civilians. Good examples of this include *Birdsong* (Sebastian Faulks), *The Return of the Soldier* (Rebecca West) and *All Quiet on the Western Front* (Erich Maria Remarque). These other novels provide a good contrast with some of the portrayals in *Strange Meeting*, together with showing how the soldiers' reactions vary.

- The reality of life on the home front was often very different to its stereotypical portrayal in the novels of the First World War. To see this topic in context, students could read *All Quiet on the Home Front* by Richard Van Emden and Steve Humphries.

Additional information and guidance on this topic, both in *Strange Meeting* and other novels, can be found in this Study Guide, in the Chapter entitled *Themes and Comparisons - The Home Front*.

(c) 'Explore the effect of Susan Hill's use of an omniscient narrator on your interpretation of *Strange Meeting*.'

- In order to tackle this subject, the student must first decide whether the use of an omniscient narrator *has* had any impact on their understanding of the novel. Remember that one of the reasons for writing this type of essay is to give a *personal* viewpoint.

- The use of third-person narrator, who is not a character in the novel makes certain aspects more complicated - unless they are handled carefully. It would be easy for an author to fall into the trap of creating situations and characters in a clumsy manner, relying too heavily on contrived conversations to make a point.

- Each student needs to examine how Susan Hill's use of narrative tools has affected their personal interpretation of this novel.

- To properly explore this topic, wider reading is essential. Novels which are written with an omniscient narrator include: *Regeneration* (Pat Barker), *Birdsong* (Sebastian Faulks) and *A Long Long Way* (Sebastian Barry). Some of these are more successful than others. Novels which have been told in the first person include: *All Quiet on the Western Front* (Erich Maria Remarque) and *Not So Quiet...* (Helen Zenna Smith). In addition, these two latter works are also written in the present tense (with the exception of the Epilogue, which is told in the third person, past tense). All of these novels provide useful contrasts and comparisons with *Strange Meeting* and reading at least two of these should enable students to form a greater depth of opinion regarding the merits of different narrative styles.

Additional information and guidance on this topic can be found in this Study Guide, in the Chapter entitled *Critical Analysis - Narrative Style*.

(d) 'Explore the ways in which Susan Hill uses letters in the novel *Strange Meeting*.'

- David Barton is the main letter-writer in the novel, although there are other pieces of correspondence which are used to achieve different effects.

- Barton's letters not only help to build his character, but also to reveal various aspects of the plot. If not handled properly, this can sometimes feel strained. Students must, therefore, examine their own interpretation of the author's use of letters as a narrative tool. Do you feel that they have been employed wisely and to great effect, or not?

- Some of Barton's letters are very long. Do you feel that the length of these can sometimes make them boring, rather than revealing interesting anecdotes of life at the front? Would the author, therefore, have been better off giving the reader shorter excerpts?

- Letters become of greater importance to Hilliard as his friendship with Barton develops. At the beginning, he thinks of letters from home only as something which 'broke the monotony' of life at the front. Barton's family, however, begin to include him in their correspondence and by the end of the novel, he is writing to them as though he knew them personally.

- Once Barton has died, the letters become a means, not only of communication, but also of solace. In this way, not only does Susan Hill use correspondence as a device within the plot, but also to show the change in her leading character's personality and temperament.

- Many other authors have used letters in their novels, with differing degrees of success. These include *A Long Long Way* (Sebastian Barry), *Birdsong* (Sebastian Faulks) and *Not So Quiet…* (Helen Zenna Smith)

Additional information and guidance on this topic can be found in this Study Guide, in the Chapter entitled *Critical Analysis - Narrative Style*.

Other possible topics...

- Students could choose to explore Susan Hill's use of **language**, possibly focusing on the notion that 'less is more' in the descriptions of battle scenes.

- An examination could be made of the methods employed to create **characters**. Susan Hill has used several, including letters, memories, reactions and description. For example, students could explore the way in which we learn about Barton compared to the methods used to show the personality of Hilliard.

CREATIVE TRANSFORMATIONAL WRITING

As the title suggests, this option gives the student more scope for creativity - within certain limitations. Here, rather than writing a piece which clinically analyses one or more aspects of the novel, you could choose to *become* the author instead. Do not be fooled into thinking that this provides you with an 'easy' option, however. Your essay MUST demonstrate that you have understood not only the content, language, structure and narrative viewpoint of the novel, but also that you have completely absorbed the author's style and purpose in writing it in the first place.

Within the restrictions of the permitted word-count and the fact that the assessment objectives remain the same, you have to adopt the style - both narrative and linguistic - of Susan Hill, retain the characterisations which she has already created, focus on the context of the novel and make your piece believable and realistic.

There are several possibilities within this choice of essay:

(a) The Epilogue

- Perhaps the most obvious choice of topic within this option. Students must remember that in her 'Afterword', even Susan Hill points out that she has no idea what would have happened to her characters as they 'live within the confines of the novel'.

- Your narrative does not necessarily need to begin with Hilliard's visit to the Bartons. You could choose to begin your epilogue at the end of the war, for instance, or perhaps even later still, provided that you find a suitable narrative device for explaining the intervening years.

- If you choose this path, bear in mind that Susan Hill has, throughout her novel, avoided clumsy methods of explanation, preferring instead, to use letters or recollections.

- You must remain in character, in terms of the writing style which you employ and the personalities you portray. Make a thorough examination of

Hilliard's character and do not give him inappropriate qualities. Think also about how the war and, in particular, Barton's death might change his character and incorporate these attributes into your narrative.

- Remember that you are acting as a third-person narrator, which gives you insight into the thoughts of all the characters you are portraying. However, pay attention to how you achieve and demonstrate this understanding, to avoid your narrative becoming contrived.

- Reading about soldiers who survived the war will be helpful in achieving a successful epilogue. One recommendation is *Siegfried Sassoon*, by Max Egremont, as the subject of this biography was not only a survivor, but was haunted and deeply affected by his wartime experiences. In addition, of course, Sassoon was also a sexually ambiguous and intensely private man.

Additional information and guidance on this topic can be found in this Study Guide, in the Chapter entitled *Character Analysis - John Hilliard*.

(b) Hilliard's Diary

- While we know that Hilliard did not keep a diary during his time in France, it is not inconceivable, given Barton's influence, that he might have considered keeping one after his injury, to help him come to terms with his losses. Alternatively, he may have been encouraged to do this by Barton's family.

- If you choose, this could be treated as a means of writing an 'Epilogue', or of giving further insight into Hilliard's thoughts about his own and/or Barton's families, Barton himself, the war, or possibly post-war contact with other survivors.

- If you show Hilliard writing about Barton, Hilliard's family or other survivors, you should study the personalities of these characters, as portrayed in the novel and adhere to the descriptions and characteristics which they have been given. Henry Partington and his son are the only people about whom little knowledge can be gained from the story, but we are made aware of Hilliard's opinion of his brother-in-law.

- If you write about Barton's family, you will have less information to work with, but this does not mean that you have an entirely free hand. The letters which are exchanged between Barton, Hilliard and Barton's family give you a reasonable insight into their personalities and there is some information about their lifestyles, careers, marriages, ages etc.

- Make yourself familiar with all of the characters (but especially Hilliard) and remember that, unlike in the remainder of the story, you will be writing in the first person - giving Hilliard's perspective only.

- Think carefully about the dates which you give in his diary and research these to ensure that you do not trip up, historically, in the time-line which you give the entries, when compared to the war itself. A good guide for this would be to look at *1914-1918: The History of the First World War* by David Stephenson or to visit www.firstworldwar.com.

- Reading diaries which were written by soldiers at the time, although many relate to war-time experiences, might also help with context and language. Recommendations include *General Jack's Diary* edited by John Terrain and *The War The Infantry Knew* by Captain J. C. Dunn

Additional information and guidance on this topic can be found in this Study Guide, in the Chapter entitled *Character Analysis*.

(c) Letters

- There has clearly been some additional correspondence between John Hilliard and the Barton family, which has not been included in the novel. In Hilliard's letter to the Barton's, he is still in France, while in her last letter, Miriam Barton is anticipating Hilliard's visit. You could, therefore, fill in the gaps, by providing some supplementary letters between the two.

- In these letters, you could give details of Hilliard's recovery. We know that he says he is 'learning to manage crutches', but further letters might give more detail. Miriam Barton says that they have 'had no further news' of David, but there may have been some, perhaps supplied by Captain Franklin, during the intervening time.

- Bearing in mind the permitted word count, and that Miriam Barton is renowned for writing fairly lengthy correspondence, you would probably only need to compose between two and four letters.

- In each case, remember that you would be writing from the perspective of the author of the letter - as well as adopting Susan Hill's narrative techniques. Therefore, you should make yourself familiar with the letters which have been given in the novel and emulate their style.

- Keep to context and character in your letter(s). So, for example, Miriam Barton may have news about her son, Dick, who we know is serving in the Royal Army Medical Corps in Egypt. Keep in mind also that the Bartons are a very open family, so Miriam might feel at liberty to discuss her daughter, Nancy's, pregnancy. How would Hilliard react to these confidences? Might his reaction now be different to when Barton was alive?

Additional information and guidance on this topic can be found in this Study Guide, in the Chapter entitled *Character Analysis*.

Other possible suggestions...

- An epilogue to the novel could also be written from the perspective of Constance or Beth Hilliard. Both of these women are intensely private, but might commit their thoughts to a diary.

- A study of the home front could take the form of an outline of the reaction to Hilliard's injury from the perspective of his family. You could conjure up the scenes as they receive news of his wounds, showing how each character responds.

- You could make a study of Captain Franklin's reaction to Barton and Hilliard. A diary would be a good means of doing this, explaining his behaviour towards them and outlining his motives.

2. COMPARATIVE WORK

Students can choose to compare, or connect, their chosen prose text with their preferred drama piece. This is only one of the options available and students may prefer to restrict their comparative piece to plays only. *Strange Meeting*, due to its focus on the human element, makes a good text to use in comparison with each of the plays. Students should bear in mind that *Strange Meeting* is a novel, intended to be read, while the plays are intended to be performed, generally, before a live audience. This can have an effect on the reader's (or audience's) interpretation of certain aspects of the piece. If you have chosen to use *Strange Meeting* as your prose text and wish to use it for comparative purposes, there are a few options as to how this could be achieved.

JOURNEY'S END and STRANGE MEETING

Students have several options here, and could easily look at any of the following topics:

Male Relationships

Here students have several options. In *Strange Meeting*, there is really only the one relationship to study: that between Barton and Hilliard. *Journey's End*, on the other hand, provides more scope, in that students could focus on either Stanhope's friendship with Osborne, or his relationship with Raleigh.

Barton and Hilliard form a close friendship based on their shared experiences, having had no previous knowledge of one another. Their initial meeting is tentative, on both sides, but it takes very little time to break down their barriers and for love to develop.

By the time the audience is introduced to Stanhope, the lead character in *Journey's End*, they are already aware that he is suffering from a dependency on alcohol and has become war-weary. In addition, however, they also know that Osborne is extremely protective and loyal towards Stanhope. This is a very different relationship from the one demonstrated in *Strange Meeting*. Osborne is significantly older than Stanhope and, as a former schoolmaster, looks upon all the officers as a father-figure. Towards Stanhope, in particular, Osborne becomes very protective.

Stanhope's relationship with Raleigh is, in some ways, more similar to the one between Barton and Hilliard. There is a greater similarity in the ages of these characters and Raleigh is a new recruit, keen to participate and rediscover his friendship with Stanhope, whom he had known at school. Stanhope's character is, in some ways, similar to Hilliard. They are both well-respected by their fellow officers, and both men are private, even introverted personalities.

Having chosen which relationships to portray, students would need to study the characters concerned, focusing on how the authors have depicted their friendships and bearing in mind the time at which each piece was written, which would have had an impact on content. Also students should bear in mind that R. C. Sherriff served as an officer during the war, while Susan Hill's novel is based on research of the time.

The Effects of War on the Individual

The two characters who would require inclusion under this topic, would be Stanhope from *Journey's End* and Barton from *Strange Meeting*. The main difference between these two is the length of time which they have spent at the front. Stanhope has been in France for three years, while Barton has only just arrived.

Stanhope's character has a strong dependency on alcohol and Osborne - who has adopted the nickname 'Uncle'. This is, however, more than just being war-weary, as Stanhope is shown to be psychologically damaged by his experiences. The changes in him are made apparent by Raleigh's reactions - as the young officer barely recognises the man he had known as a sporting hero at school. However, when his old schoolfriend Raleigh lies dying, Stanhope becomes the hero once more, consoling his friend in his final moments, before going up into the trenches, to face his own death.

Barton, on the other hand, as a new recruit, initially represents innocence and a keen sense of adventure. As time progresses and he witnesses more of the war, Barton loses both of these qualities, becoming frightened by his own reactions and fearful that the war will forever change him.

Although these authors have portrayed two different reactions to war, they demonstrate that each individual behaved and responded differently. Students would need to study each of the characters, including their backgrounds, and assess the realism of their reactions, both in terms of context and the personalities themselves.

The Effects of Death

In both of these texts, one can see the impact which the death of one character has on the survivors. In the case of *Journey's End*, the obvious subject for this is the death of Osborne. This takes place during a raid, which achieves little, but carries a high price for the officers in the dugout, who have lost their beloved 'Uncle'. Stanhope's reaction to Osborne's death is anger - both at the pointless raid, and at Raleigh, who had been with Osborne at the time.

In *Strange Meeting*, students could look at the death of Coulter. In itself, this episode might seem insignificant, but the reactions of the characters who survive is the interesting aspect. Barton blames himself for Coulter's death and is haunted by the question of whether he had really died instantly or been left alive, but dying, in No Man's Land. Hilliard, on the other hand, is angry with Barton, feeling that he may have caused the problem in the first place, by going too close to the German trenches and giving away their position.

As well as looking at the reaction of the survivors, students should also focus on the character of the dead soldier and their significance to the plot. Osborne clearly has an important part to play in Stanhope's life, while Coulter is, perhaps, less crucial to Barton or Hilliard, although both men seem fond of him.

NOT ABOUT HEROES and STRANGE MEETING

Below are some of the possible themes or topics which students could choose to study:

The Portrayal of Male Relationships

Not About Heroes is a play, based entirely on the friendship which formed between Siegfried Sassoon and Wilfred Owen, while they were both at Craiglockhart Military Hospital in Edinburgh during the summer of 1917 and which ended with the death of Owen on 4th November 1918. As such, their friendship has similar foundations to the one between Barton and Hilliard, in that neither man personally knew the other before they met - although Owen had heard of Sassoon as a poet - and they were thrown together in unusual circumstances. In addition the characters involved share some similar qualities.

Hilliard and Barton are shown to have little in common, Barton being from a fairly middle-class background, where he can be open and frank with his family. Hilliard, on the other hand comes from a restricted and prim environment, where emotions are kept in check at all times. Their meeting proves pivotal for both characters.

Similarly, Owen came from a conventional background and shared a very close and honest relationship with his mother, in particular. Sassoon's upbringing had been similar to Hilliard's and his relationship with his family, while not so strained, could certainly not be called 'open'. The meeting between these two characters, as portrayed in the play, proved to be possibly more important for Owen, than for Sassoon.

In studying the growing relationships involved, students should also focus on the background and development of the four characters. Bearing in mind that Sassoon and Owen were real people, reading good biographies of the two would be useful. Among the best are *Siegfried Sassoon* by Max Egremont and *Wilfred Owen: A New Biography* by Dominic Hibberd.

The Effects of War on the Individual

Both Owen and Sassoon have become affected by their experiences in the war, to different extents, but with the same consequences. Owen is portrayed in the play *Not About Heroes* as an extremely shy and nervous young man, for whom the experience of war has proved too much. He has, therefore, been sent to Craiglockhart to recover from his neurosis. The reason behind Sassoon's presence at the military hospital, had nothing really to do with conventional shell-shock, but was related to his Declaration against the continuation of the war itself. However, there is no denying that Sassoon had also become affected by the war.

In *Strange Meeting*, Hilliard is portrayed as war-weary, but glad to be returning to the front. This actually says more about his home life than about his war experiences, although we are given glimpses of his fears. Barton shows his feelings more easily than Hilliard and becomes deeply troubled by various events which happen during his time in France.

The portrayals in *Strange Meeting* are completely fictitious - although that does not make them unrealistic. Those of Sassoon and Owen in *Not About Heroes* are based in reality. Students could, therefore, focus on the different ways in which both authors have presented these aspects, paying attention to the context and realism involved.

THE ACCRINGTON PALS and STRANGE MEETING

There are several possible themes which students could choose to study in this section of their coursework studies, most of which also incorporate an in-depth analysis of the characters involved.

The Home Front

Strange Meeting begins on the home front and, throughout the novel, there are reminders of the attitudes of those at home. *The Accrington Pals*, on the other hand, is set almost entirely on the home front and is told from the perspective of the people left behind with the town's men go off to war.

In *Strange Meeting*, Hilliard's family are seen to demonstrate a someone callous and complacent attitude to the war and to their son's participation. The Major, an old family friend, is equally arrogant, believing that he understands the war better than Hilliard, because he is a former soldier himself. These portrayals are fairly stereotypical and are contrasted with those of Barton's family, which we discover through the correspondence which passes between them and David Barton.

The civilians in *The Accrington Pals* have different attitudes to the war and to the mens' participation. Some are almost pleased to see the men depart, while others worry.

Both of these texts were written in the second half of the twentieth century, presenting a view of the home front, based on research rather than experience. Students should focus on the success of these portrayals, their context and the social class of the characters involved, possibly using a book such as *All Quiet on the Home Front* (Van Emden and Humphries), for reference.

The Role of Women

Women are represented very differently in these two texts, mainly because the social backgrounds and lifestyles of the two sets of women differ greatly.

In *The Accrington Pals*, the characters are all working-class. The women who are left behind are forced to become the bread-winners in their household and, in some cases, cope with children and the household as well as working outside of the home. Their jobs vary, but many change their occupation and undertake war-work, or take over the jobs which the men would have done before they went to war. Almost all of the women portrayed in *The Accrington Pals* are strong and self-reliant, but they are capable of expressing their emotions and discussing their feelings with their friends.

Strange Meeting could not be more different. The characters of Constance and Beth Hilliard are upper-class and do not work outside of the home at all. Both of them have undertaken some war work, although this is hardly strenuous, taking the form of knitting socks and mittens for the soldiers.

Setting, therefore, is of great significance to these portrayals. Students should focus, therefore, on the social backgrounds of the women involved and how the war affected their situations and their status. Good background and contextual reference can be found in *British Culture and The First World War* by George Robb.

FURTHER READING RECOMMENDATIONS FOR STUDENTS

Students are often expected to demonstrate a sound knowledge of the texts which they are studying and also to enhance this knowledge with extensive reading of other books within this genre. I have provided on the following pages a list of books, poetry, plays and non-fiction which, in my opinion, provide a good basic understanding of this topic. In addition, a small review of each book has been provided to help students choose which of the following are most suitable for them. Those marked with an 'A' are, in my opinion, suitable only for students of A-Level and above.

NOVELS

BIRDSONG by Sebastian Faulks

Written in 1993, this novel tells the story of Stephen Wraysford, his destructive pre-war love-affair, his war experiences and, through the eyes of his grand-daughter, the effects of the war on his personality and his generation. A central theme to this story is man's ability to overcome adversity: to rise above his circumstances and survive - no matter what is thrown in his path. Many readers find the first part of this novel difficult to get through, but it is worth persevering. The pre-war section of the novel is essential in the understanding of Stephen Wraysford's character and his reactions to the events which happen later. Faulks's descriptions of battle scenes are among the best in this genre. In our view, this novel is suitable only for A-Level students, due to some adult themes.

A VERY LONG ENGAGEMENT by Sebastien Japrisot

A story of enduring love, truth and determination. Refusing to believe that her fiancé can possibly have left her forever, Mathilde decides to search for Manech whom she has been told is missing, presumed dead. She learns from a first-hand witness, that he may not have died, so she sets out on a voyage of discovery - learning not just about his fate, but also a great deal about herself and human nature. Mathilde herself has to overcome her own personal fears and hardships and, out of sheer persistence and a refusal to accept the obvious, she eventually discovers the truth. Although this novel does not form part of the main syllabus reading list, it does make an interesting and fairly easy read and is useful from the perspective that it gives a French woman's viewpoint of the war.

REGENERATION by Pat Barker

This book is, as its title implies, a novel about the rebuilding of men following extreme trauma. Billy Prior is a young working-class officer - a 'temporary gentleman' - who finds himself at Craiglockhart Military Hospital in Edinburgh, having been damaged by his experiences on the Western Front. It is the job of Dr W. H. R. Rivers, to 'mend' Prior, and others like him, ready for them to return to the fighting, while wrestling with his own conscience at the same time. Interweaved into this central plot is the meeting, also at Craiglockhart, of poets Siegfried Sassoon and Wilfred Owen, who are both there to receive treatment. This mixture of fact and fiction within a novel has created some controversy, but it is a common feature within this genre and one which Pat Barker handles better than most. This is an immensely useful book - even if not read as part of the Trilogy - as it takes place away from the front lines, showing the reader the deep and long-lasting effects of battle upon men, whose lives would never be the same again. Due to some adult content, we recommend this book for A-Level students only.

THE RETURN OF THE SOLDIER by Rebecca West

Written in 1918, by an author who had lived through the conflict, this home-front novel gives a useful insight into the trauma of war and society's reaction, as seen through the eyes of three women. Chris Baldry, an officer and husband of Kitty, returns home mid-way through the war, suffering from shell-shock and amnesia. He believes that that he is still in a relationship with Margaret Allington - his first love from fifteen years earlier. Kitty, Margaret and Chris's cousin, Jenny, must decide whether to leave Chris in his make-believe world, safe from the war; or whether to 'cure' him and risk his future welfare once he returns to being a soldier. A useful novel from many perspectives in that it was written right at the end of the war, and it gives a female, home-front view of the effects of the war on individuals and families.

ALL QUIET ON THE WESTERN FRONT by Erich Maria Remarque

Written from first-hand experience of life in the trenches, this novel is the moving account of the lives of a group of young German soldiers during the First World War. Remarque had been in the trenches during the later stages of the war and this poignant account of war is a must-read for all those who show an interest in this subject. His descriptions of trench-life and battles are second-to-none and his portrayal of the close friendships forged between the men make this an immensely valuable piece of literature. The fact that this, often shocking, story is told from a German perspective also demonstrates the universal horrors of the war and the sympathy between men of both sides for others enduring the same hardships as themselves.

A LONG LONG WAY by Sebastian Barry

Sebastian Barry's novel tells the a story of Willie Dunne, a young Irish volunteer serving in the trenches of the Western Front. Willie must not only contend with the horrors of the war, but also his own confused feelings regarding the Easter uprising of 1916, and his father's disapproval. Willie's feelings and doubts lead to great upheavals in his life, including personal losses and betrayals by those whom he had believed he could trust. This is an interesting novel about loyalty, war and love, although it does suffer from a degree of historical inaccuracy. In our opinion, due to the adult content of this novel, it is suitable only for A-Level students.

NOT SO QUIET... by Helen Zenna Smith

This novel describes the lives of women working very close to the front line on the Western Front during the First World War, as ambulance drivers. Theirs is a dangerous job, in harsh conditions, with little or no respite. Helen (or Smithy, as she is called by her friends), eventually breaks down under the pressure of the work and returns, briefly, to England. An excellent novel for studying the female perspective, as well as the home front.

POETRY

It is recommended that students read from a wide variety of poets, including female writers. The following anthologies provide good resources for students.

POEMS OF THE FIRST WORLD WAR -
NEVER SUCH INNOCENCE
Edited by Martin Stephen

Probably one of the finest anthologies of First World War poetry currently available. Martin Stephen has collected together some of the best known works by some of the most famous and well-read poets and mixed these with more obscure verses, including many by women and those on the home-front, together with some popular songs both from home and from the front. These have been interspersed with excellent notes which give the reader sufficient information without being too weighty. At the back of the book, there are short biographical notes on many of the poets. This is a fine anthology, suitable both for those who are starting out with their studies, and for the more experienced reader.

LADS: LOVE POETRY OF THE TRENCHES by Martin Taylor

Featuring many lesser-known poets and poems, this anthology approaches the First World War from a different perspective: love. A valuable introduction discusses the emotions of men who, perhaps for the first time, were discovering their own capacity to love their fellow man. This is not an anthology of purely homo-erotic poems, but also features verses by those who had found affection and deep, lasting friendship in the trenches of the First World War.

SCARS UPON MY HEART
Selected by Catherine Reilly

First published in 1981, this anthology is invaluable as it features a collection of poems written exclusively by women on the subject of the First World War. Some of the better known female poets are featured here, such as Vera Brittain and Jessie Pope, but there are also many more writers who are less famous. In addition there are some poets whose work is featured, who are not now renowned for their poetry, but for their works in other areas of literature. Many of the poets included here have minor biographical details featured at the end of the anthology. This book has become the 'standard' for those wishing to study the female contribution to this genre.

UP THE LINE TO DEATH
Edited by Brian Gardner

This anthology, described by its editor Brian Gardner as a 'book about war', is probably, and deservedly, one of the most widely read in this genre. The famous and not-so-famous sit happily together within in these pages of carefully selected poetry. Arranged thematically, these poems provide a poet's-eye-view of the progression of the war, from the initial euphoria and nationalistic pride of John Freeman's 'Happy is England Now' to Sassoon's plea that we should 'never forget'. Useful biographical details and introductions complete this book, which is almost certainly the most useful and important of all the First World War poetry anthologies.

NON-FICTION

UNDERTONES OF WAR by Edmund Blunden

Edmund Blunden's memoir of his experiences in the First World War is a moving, enlightening and occasionally humorous book, demonstrating above all the intense feelings of respect and comradeship which Blunden found in the trenches.

MEMOIRS OF AN INFANTRY OFFICER by Siegfried Sassoon

Following on from *Memoirs of a Fox-hunting Man*, this book is an autobiographical account of Sassoon's life during the First World War. Sassoon has changed the names of the characters and George Sherston (Sassoon) is not a poet. Sassoon became one of the war's most famous poets and this prose account of his war provides useful background information. (For a list of the fictional characters and their factual counterparts, see Appendix II of *Siegfried Sassoon* by John Stuart Roberts.)

THE GREAT WAR GENERALS ON THE WESTERN FRONT 1914-1918 by Robin Neillands

Like many others before and since, the cover of this book claims that it will dismiss the old myth that the troops who served in the First World War were badly served by their senior officers. Unlike most of the other books, however, this one is balanced and thought-provoking. Of particular interest within this book is the final chapter which provides an assessment of the main protagonists and their role in the conflict.

THE WESTERN FRONT by Richard Holmes

This is one of many history books about the First World War. Dealing specifically with the Western Front, Richard Holmes looks at the creation of the trench warfare system, supplying men and munitions, major battles and living on the front line..

LETTERS FROM A LOST GENERATION (FIRST WORLD WAR LETTERS OF VERA BRITTAIN AND FOUR FRIENDS) Edited by Alan Bishop and Mark Bostridge

A remarkable insight into the changes which the First World War caused to a particular set of individuals. In this instance, Vera Brittain lost four important people in her life (two close friends, her fiancé and her brother). The agony this evoked is demonstrated through letters sent between these five characters, which went on to form the basis of Vera Brittain's autobiography *Testament of Youth*.

1914-1918: VOICES AND IMAGES OF THE GREAT WAR
by Lyn MacDonald

One of the most useful 'unofficial' history books available to those studying the First World War. This book tells the story of the soldiers who fought the war through their letters, diary extracts, newspaper reports, poetry and eye-witness accounts. As with all of Lyn MacDonald's excellent books, *Voices and Images of the Great War* tells its story through the words of the people who were there. The author gives just the right amount of background information of a political and historical nature to keep the reader interested and informed, while leaving the centre-stage to those who really matter... the men themselves.

BIBLIOGRAPHY

STRANGE MEETING by Susan Hill

BIRDSONG by Sebastian Faulks

ALL QUIET ON THE WESTERN FRONT by Erich Maria Remarque

THE RETURN OF THE SOLDIER by Rebecca West

JOURNEY'S END by R C Sherriff

REGENERATION by Pat Barker

THE EYE IN THE DOOR by Pat Barker

THE GHOST ROAD by Pat Barker

A LONG LONG WAY by Sebastian Barry

THE ACCRINGTON PALS by Peter Whelan

NOT ABOUT HEROES by Stephen MacDonald

UNDERTONES OF WAR by Edmund Blunden

SIEGFRIED'S JOURNEY by Siegfried Sassoon

MEMOIRS OF AN INFANTRY OFFICER by Siegfried Sassoon

TWELVE DAYS ON THE SOMME by Sidney Rogerson

THE LAST OF THE EBB by Sidney Rogerson

GENERAL JACK'S DIARY edited by John Terrain

ALL QUIET ON THE HOME FRONT by Richard Van Emden and Steve Humphries

BRITISH CULTURE AND THE FIRST WORLD WAR by George Robb

SIEGFRIED SASSOON by Max Egremont

UP THE LINE TO DEATH by Brian Gardner

LADS - LOVE POETRY OF THE TRENCHES by Martin Taylor

OTHER GREAT WAR LITERATURE STUDY GUIDE TITLES

GREAT WAR LITERATURE STUDY GUIDE PAPERBACKS:

Title	ISBN
A Long Long Way A-Level Study Guide	978-1905378401
All Quiet on the Western Front	978-1905378302
Birdsong A-Level Study Guide	978-1905378449
Journey's End - GCSE	978-1905378371
Journey's End - A-Level	978-1905378401
Regeneration A-Level Study Guide	978-1905378395
The Return of the Soldier	978-1905378357
Female Poets of the First World War - Vol.1	978-1905378258
War Poets of the First World War - Vol.1	978-1905378241
War Poets of the First World War - Vol.2	978-1905378425
First World War Plays	978-1905378418

GREAT WAR LITERATURE STUDY GUIDE E-BOOKS:

NOVELS & PLAYS

A Long Long Way
All Quiet on the Western Front
Journey's End (A-Level or GCSE)
Regeneration
Strange Meeting
The Return of the Soldier
The Accrington Pals
Not About Heroes
Oh What a Lovely War

POET BIOGRAPHIES AND POETRY ANALYSIS:

Harold Begbie
Edmund Blunden
Rupert Brooke
May Wedderburn Cannan
Margaret Postgate Cole
Nancy Cunard
Eleanor Farjeon
Gilbert Frankau
Wilfrid Wilson Gibson
Robert Graves
Julian Grenfell
Ivor Gurney
Alan P Herbert
W N Hodgson
Geoffrey Anketell Studdert Kennedy
E A Mackintosh
John McCrae
Charlotte Mew
Edith Nesbit
Robert Nichols

Wilfred Owen
Jessie Pope
Isaac Rosenberg
Siegfried Sassoon
Charles Hamilton Sorley
Edward Wyndham Tennant
Edward Thomas
Iris Tree
Katharine Tynan Hinkson
Robert Ernest Vernède
Arthur Graeme West

Please note that e-books are only available direct from our Web site at www.greatwarliterature.co.uk and cannot be purchased through bookshops.